PEAS & QUEUES

THE MINEFIELD OF MODERN MANNERS

SANDI TOKSVIG

P

PROFILE BOOKS

This paperback edition published in 2014

First published in Great Britain in 2013 by
PROFILE BOOKS LTD
3A Exmouth House
Pine Street
London EC1R 0JH
www.profilebooks.com

1 3 5 7 9 10 8 6 4 2

Printed and bound in Great Britain by
CPI Group (UK) Ltd, Croydon CR0 4YY

A CIP catalogue record for this book is available from the British Library.

ISBN 978 1 78125 033 4
eISBN 978 1 84765 866 1

for Mary

CONTENTS

TO THE READER

In 1530 when Erasmus of Rotterdam wrote his book on manners, *De civilitate morum puerilium* (On Civility in Boys), he directed his advice to the eleven-year-old son of the Prince of Veere, Henry of Burgundy. The instructions were in Latin. I follow in his footsteps by addressing this volume to a delightful child in my life called Mary. She is eight at present. This is not a book for children, but she and I have had many conversations about manners. Her behaviour is splendid, but nevertheless one day she may need a volume to reach for as matters arise in her life. I hope as she becomes a grown-up that this is it. It is impossible to imagine every type of encounter or situation which a person might face so I have stuck to the most general ones in the order most likely to occur. Although Mary was the inspiration for this book I hope it will also prove useful to anyone not planning to live as a hermit. I have made it easier for her (and you) by not using Latin (very much).

TO BEGIN: AN INTRODUCTION

WHY DO WE NEED GOOD MANNERS?

Nobody knows the age of the human race, but everybody
agrees that it is old enough to know better.

Author unknown

Dear Mary

This bit of a book is usually referred to as 'The Introduction'.
It's the section most likely to be skipped by a reader so you may
wonder why the author bothered. If you do just want to crack on
with the basics of manners then by all means move along, but if
you want to know why you should pay attention to them at all
then it might be interesting. At any rate do be polite enough to at
least give it a go, seeing as I've made the effort to write it.

Sit up straight? How annoying

Two points straight away:

The first thing to say is that basic manners apply no matter
where you are or what you are doing. They are even a good idea
when no one is watching. Having a code of behaviour will help
you know how to react to the unexpected.

The second point is to assure you that manners are not some

new notion invented by the present generation of old fogies to annoy youngsters. The fact is that, on the whole, human beings don't live in isolation from each other nor do they want to. Think how delighted Robinson Crusoe was when Man Friday turned up. If we're not going to live alone on a desert island then we need to find ways to get on. Irritatingly we can't all just do what we like. Imagine the chaos there would be on the roads. Manners are simply an expression of how we manage the tricky art of co-existing. A good starting point for this is to show kindness and consideration to others and every society has and has had some basic notion about this.

Most religions have spent a lot of time working out how you ought to behave and most of them have what is known as

The Golden Rule

For example, the Mahabharata of Hinduism declares, 'This is the sum of duty; do naught unto others what would cause pain if done to you', while the Jewish Talmud instructs 'What is hateful to you, do not do to your fellowman. This is the entire Law; all the rest is commentary' and the Christian Bible follows on with 'Thou shalt love thy neighbour as thyself'. Sounds a simple plan which, if you follow it, should set you off on the right foot.

MANNERS MAKETH THE MAN (AND THE WOMAN, THE KID, THE DOG . . .)

A man's manners are a mirror in which he shows his portrait.

Johann Wolfgang von Goethe (1749–1832), German writer

The general notion is that how you are seen to behave says something about the kind of person you are. Worrying about what impact your behaviour has on other people means you are thinking about someone other than yourself. It's not about using the right fork or addressing royalty correctly, it's about doing your best to be a considerate member of the community. We have rules because predictable behaviour can be very comforting. It is nice to know what to do if you attend an event, which is why there are so many helpful hints about things like formal dinners, works functions, weddings and funerals. These are stages in life which will come up for us all and it's good to have a game plan.

Minding your Ps and Qs

The expression 'mind your Ps and Qs', meaning 'be on your best behaviour', has been around for so long that no one can quite recall where it came from. There are many candidates:

1. It was a foreshortened admonishment to children to remember to say *Please* and *Thank you*.

2. It was a seventeenth-century admonishment for drinkers to keep an eye on how many pints and quarts they consumed.

3. It was an eighteenth-century admonishment for sailors to pay attention to their *peas* (a sailor's pea coat) and *queues* (a traditional nautical ponytail).

I could carry on through history seeking a meaning via the Norman Invasion of 1066, specific reading symbols in Medieval Latin texts or how early printers might easily confuse lowercase Ps and Qs but we have too much to do to get sidetracked. The fact that we don't know the precise origin of the phrase seems appropriate, for 'minding your Ps and Qs' at all is far from an exact science.

Writing the rules

It's important to understand that rules about manners are not laws. They're not really even rules. They are suggestions. You don't have to keep them but you may get along better in life if you do. Over the years there have been many attempts to write down propositions for behaviour to help grease the wheels of the great social machine. Probably the book most responsible for kicking off modern ideas about this was the book I mentioned right at the outset – *De civilitate morum puerilium* (On Civility in

Boys) – which was written in 1530 by Erasmus of Rotterdam. (He also wrote *The Handbook for the Christian Knight* and the rather jollier *In Praise of Folly* in which Folly mucks about as a goddess having been brought up by two nymphs called *Inebriation* and *Ignorance* but sadly we haven't the time.) Quite what it was about sixteenth-century boys in Rotterdam that required a whole volume of suggestions for better behaviour is hard to know, but in the first six years of the book's publication it was reprinted thirty times. The first English version came out in 1532 and from then on it became popular to instruct young people in the basics of civil behaviour.

Erasmus didn't invent the idea of good conduct. You find it written about as soon as you find writing of any kind in history. There is a papyrus in the Bibliothèque Nationale in Paris from the Egyptian Fifth Dynasty (c. 2414–2375 BC) called *The Maxims of Ptahhotep* which is said to have been written by one of the top officials to King Isesi. It is low on jokes but in it Ptahhotep recommends the sort of behaviour that still seems quite a good idea today – truthfulness, self-control, and kindness to others.

EVOLVING ETIQUETTE

I mention the past but it's critical not to get stuck in it. The way manners are expressed evolves on an almost daily basis. In the twelfth century, for example, it was recommended that one should cough very loudly when entering a house 'for there may be something doing which you ought not to see'. These days it's easier to ring the bell.

The word 'Etiquette' derives from the French word for small labels or tickets attached to bags to tell you what was inside them. In the same way 'Protocol' comes from the Greek *proto-kollon* which was a sheet glued to a manuscript case to show its contents. Labels or stickers attached to things proclaiming what they were and where they belonged gradually developed into written instructions for how to behave. They would be posted, for example, outside a soldier's billet or lodging to tell him what was expected. Interestingly, in Danish the word 'billet' means 'ticket' just like 'etiquette'. Those who ran Louis XIV's palace at Versailles used *étiquettes* (little cards) to remind courtiers to keep off the grass or whatever else was considered *de rigueur* in court life.

In fact a lot of the words associated with manners have their origins in the royal courts of the past. The word 'courteous' even has 'court' in it. It starts popping up in the mid fourteenth century and comes from the Old French *curteis* – 'having courtly bearing or manners'. The German word *hübsch* meaning 'beautiful' is descended from *hofesch* with the word *hof* meaning 'court'. Presumably the notion was that only the rich had time to behave really well and the poor should at least aspire to follow their example.

What is and isn't generally acceptable changes all the time. There is a painting by the Dutchman Andries Both called *Hunting lice by candlelight*. It was painted in 1630 and it shows four men engaged in ridding a kneeling figure of unwanted vermin in his hair. This is not a procedure most people today would think of as an acceptable public practice. When I was at boarding school in the late 1970s my headmistress would have had a polite but clear seizure if any one of us girls had turned up in church without white gloves on. Fortunately (although not for the white glove industry) that is a notion which has died a happy death.

There are rules today about Twitter and Facebook which didn't exist a decade ago because neither did Twitter or Facebook. Modes of behaviour need to be examined continuously as we decide which are worth keeping and which need to be updated. That doesn't mean that some rules which have been around for a long time aren't still worth sticking to.

SOCIAL HIERARCHY

An Englishman's way of speaking absolutely classifies him,
The moment he talks he makes some other Englishman despise him.

My Fair Lady, Alan Jay Lerner, 1956

Before we get going let me just be very clear that having good manners has nothing to do with class. Being polite is not the same as being subservient. Fortunately we no longer live in a world where anyone needs to tug a forelock. Respect needs to be earned whatever your background and it is not something anyone should assume they will receive because of their social class. Sadly, there are some who have failed to notice this democratisation of society and who continue to behave as if their class has any bearing on how people ought to treat them.

I have a lesbian friend who came out to her mother who was rather grand. It went better than expected, so with some trepidation my friend went on to describe her girlfriend, Frances.

'What does Frances's father do?' asked her mother.

'He used to work in a mill,' my friend replied.

'He owned a mill?' said her mother.

'No,' explained my friend, 'he was on the shop floor.'

There was a sharp intake of breath from the mother who, in her most horrified voice, exclaimed 'Frances is working class?' The lesbian thing was fine. The class thing was a complete horror.

A class act

So where class is concerned be a little cautious and

1. Never presume you know someone's background because of their accent

My English accent sounds very 'posh' but in fact I am the daughter of a journalist. I don't come from money, just another country.

2. Don't presume someone's accent is linked to their intelligence

Brain power is never measured in vowels.

3. Don't limit anyone because of the accident of their birth

Oprah Winfrey is sometimes suggested to be the most influential woman in the world. She was born to a single, poor, teenage mum in rural Mississippi.

4. Don't be a snob

This applies not just to those who think themselves in a higher class bracket but to those from the 'working' class too. It is terrible when a privileged person is arrogant but it is equally unpleasant when someone from a poor background believes that they alone have the right to know what it is to suffer.

5. Do remember the sixteenth-century French writer, Michel de Montaigne

Michel is claimed as the Father of Modern Scepticism which I'm not sure about, but he did quite rightly point out: 'However high a man sits, he still sits on his own arse.'

The upside of manners

The fact is you will do better in life if other people like you and find you are a pleasure to have around; if you know how to behave. A study by Barbara Griffin, a psychologist at the University of Western Sydney, has shown that bad manners are bad for business. It makes sense. If managers are rude to their staff then no one feels particularly inspired to work hard. If business people are rude, their customers will take their custom elsewhere.

If you find it hard to think about others then you may bear in mind that consideration for your fellow man may also be best for you. A friend of mine was a doctor at the A & E department of a large hospital. One night he was running to work and was desperate to be excused. The pubs were just closing and he ran into one to ask the landlord if he might use the facilities. 'No,' said the landlord and very rudely told him to go away. My friend explained that he was in some pain and was desperate but nevertheless the landlord threw him out. A few hours later, early in the morning, my doctor friend was called to attend a man who had broken his leg. He pulled back the curtain to a cubicle to reveal the same pub landlord. My friend smiled. He examined the man's leg. 'It's definitely broken,' he said, 'you must be in some pain. I bet you want my help but I am very busy.' My friend said he was ashamed but he made the man wait. The moral of the story? Being nice for its own sake is best, but if you can't manage that then be nice because you never know when you might need some help yourself.

AN ARIA OF ATTITUDE - THE TOP Cs OF MANNERS

Consideration
Common sense
Context
Comfort

In this book I have tried to cover situations which might arise during the general course of your life. I can only hope that I am able to provide a helpful thought. Please accept that I may be wrong in some instances (although it would be poor behaviour to make me feel bad by pointing it out). It is, of course, not possible for me to cover everything, but the plan is to lay down some basics and to make you think. After that, like a tenor singing Verdi, you need reach for your Top Cs to see you through.

The first is 'Consideration', but after that you need to remember 'Common sense' and 'Context'. Be kind, be sensible and remember that not everyone thinks or feels the way you do. Manners are there to be interpreted and common sense should always prevail. It may be considered rude to bang a perfect stranger on the back, but not if they are choking to death. We should also recall that manners change according to cultural context. What is polite to us may seem the height of bad manners to the Masai farmer whose behaviour in turn might shock the Chinese businessman who could easily upset the French drag queen who … oh, you get the picture.

The final C is 'Comfort'. In any given situation the aim of good manners should be to make as many people feel as comfortable as possible. I think probably the greatest lesson in good manners I ever heard was told to me by the photographer, Patrick Lichfield. Patrick was a member of the British aristocracy and one night in Copenhagen he was invited to have dinner with the Danish King, Frederick IX. In those days a gentleman wore a shirt with no collar, on top of which was placed a separate stiff shirt front, a detachable collar and stiff cuffs. Patrick was a little impecunious and had no clean shirt. Instead, he simply put on the shirt front and cuffs underneath his dinner jacket. No one would have known but, as luck would have it, it was a particularly warm evening and after the meal the gentlemen gathered to have brandy and cigars. As they sat down the king declared that the men 'might remove their jackets'. Patrick was mortified. He knew that manners dictated he should do as the king asked but he had no shirt on. Ready for the social disgrace he removed his jacket. The king took one look at him and immediately said, 'Splendid idea! Shirts as well' and promptly removed his shirt. Soon all the men were sitting bare-chested and Patrick was made to feel as though nothing untoward had occurred. How delighted I am that it was a Dane who behaved so well.

WHERE TO BEGIN?

All the world's a stage,
And all the men and women merely players

William Shakespeare, *As You Like It* (1599/1600)

When the Russian theatre director, Konstantin Stanislavski, developed his techniques of acting he talked a lot about the 'circles of attention'. He developed a concept of three basic circles which actors should adjust their performance to – a small, very intimate one in which we live alone or with our nearest and dearest; a medium one in which we interact with our friends and associates; and a large public one where we encounter everyone else. These circles exist in everyday life and we learn manners so that we know how to behave on each of the various stages on which we play out our existence. Usually we take our first steps within the smallest circle, so let's begin at home.

Are you ready? Off we go.

Much love
Sandi

1: AT HOME

Home is where the heart is.

Pliny the Elder (AD 23–79), Roman author

Dear Mary

I like the word 'home' partly because it has Nordic roots. The Danish equivalent is '*hjem*' and it just means where we live. It's a small word for something that means so much. For many of us the word 'home' represents the place where we grew up. If you've ever been away and been 'homesick' then you know what a powerful feeling you can have about your particular spot on earth. The fact that the quote above was written by a man in toga times shows yet again how little humans have really changed over the centuries. Of course, it's worth bearing in mind that Pliny never married or had children so he may not have known what a noisy, crowded place a home can be.

Dorothy in *The Wizard of Oz* knew that there was 'No place like home' and ideally it's the place where everyone should be at their most relaxed. This might lead you to think that it is the one location where you don't need to worry about manners. In fact the opposite is true. The people with whom you share your living space are those with whom you live most intimately, whether it's your family or your flat- or housemates. You need to respect each other and be thoughtful, or pretty soon everyone will be wishing they were living alone. How and where you live changes as you grow but the basics apply throughout your life. Even if you do live alone you are unlikely to escape having neighbours and certain rules still help everyone rub along.

Some homes are more packed with people than others, but everyone is entitled to some privacy. What you'll find is if you allow your nearest and dearest a little private space then they are more likely to do the same for you. We all have moments when we would like to be alone so there are some simple ways forward. Ideally you start with having respect for...

THE FAMILY HOME

1. Each other

It's the old 'do as you would be done by' leitmotif of manners. Parents often go on about wishing their children had more respect, but it may be that they haven't considered what a two-way street that is. Respect is something you earn. Losing your temper and shouting at those you live with is rarely a good way forward. Very little is ever achieved. Be thoughtful and attentive to everyone in the home and you will find that they will be thoughtful and attentive back. That means parents listening to the kids as well as vice versa.

That doesn't mean the kids shouldn't consider...

2. Age and experience

Annoying, I know, but quite often people who have been around for a few years have learnt a thing or two. Advice from parents or grandparents might be worth listening to. If you are a younger person living at home then consider what is being provided for you at little or no cost to you.

If you want more control of how a home runs then ask for a meeting, or plan towards the day when you have your own home.

3. The private space

Everyone has a place where they keep private things. It might be a small box with keepsakes, a money box, a diary or a desk. No matter how tempted you are to take a peek you need to hold back or you will soon find your own possessions being rummaged through by other people. Private space includes letters. The post is addressed to an individual for a reason – it's personal. You should only read letters if they are addressed to you or you have been asked to. Postcards are fair game or they would be in an envelope.

4. The closed door

If someone has closed a door in the house and is on the other side they probably did it on purpose. Perhaps they need a moment in the bathroom, perhaps there is a bedroom activity taking place which is none of your business or, amazingly, they just may want a quiet moment to think. Knock and wait till you are asked to come in.

LIVING WITH FRIENDS

There comes a time in some young people's lives when they leave home in order to go and make a life away from the family. I say 'some' because these days not everyone departs, but it is not uncommon to go from living at home to having to share a place with people of your own age. Even those who leave school and go straight into employment are unlikely to be lucky enough to have their own place. Sadly, the world has changed and many grown-ups have had the bad manners to wreck the financial system for the next generation. I was able to put down a deposit on my first flat when I was twenty-three, but the current estimate is that by the end of the decade the average age of a first-time buyer will be forty.

So if you can't afford to live alone, or don't want to, you need to find ways to get along. The basics aren't so very different to living with your family, except that you're probably less of a unit when you share with your pals and may live more independently than you would at home. Nevertheless you are still living within the small circle of existence with each other and you need to find a way to make that work.

1. Eat your own food

It's actually called stealing if you take or use someone's things without asking. The lazy person who hasn't bothered to stock up on food deserves to be hungry. You don't have to label every item of food. Just agree on a shelf each and leave it at that.

If you share some foodstuffs such as milk and you have used the last of it, get some more.

One of the best ways to ensure harmony in the house is to prepare and eat at least an occasional meal with everyone, or at least have the occasional trip to the pub or go on an outing together.

2. Clean up after yourself

Don't let your plate of food go mouldy just because you can't be bothered to clean up. Unless your mother has tracked you down and moved in you need to do your own washing-up. Do not expect that someone in your house will do it for you. Don't leave your unwashed things in the kitchen sink so no one else can clean their own.

Try to share the housework. No one wants to do it and the cleaning fairy rarely shows up. Hoover every so often and your housemates may do the same. Maybe make a rota to ensure fairness.

Do I need to say this? My daughter tells me she's had flatmates vomit after a drinking session and leave it. Really?

You need an exceptional reason not to clear away your own rubbish. In 2004 Jack Kirby was an art and design student in Hertfordshire who liked Budweiser beer. Over a three-year period he drank 5,000 cans of the lager and never got rid of the empties. The reason was perfectly reasonable. He used them to build a brilliant, life-size model of a 1965 Ford Mustang. Fortunately the car has no engine so there was no risk of anyone drinking and driving.

3. Consider your noise levels

Whatever you get up to in your own room it is important to recall that you are not living by yourself. So I'm going to suggest that you don't watch or react to porn very loudly even in your own room. This is probably not the book to suggest that if you are watching a lot of porn on your own you might want to think about that. If you have torn yourself away from watching 'Cycle Sluts' or whatever then I'm sorry there aren't more pictures but well done for making a start …

In general your extracurricular bedroom activities are not a radio show for everyone else's enjoyment. Being forced to listen to other people's private pleasure is the right recipe for an awkward situation. Consider whether you would enjoy listening to them. Be especially conscious of this if one of your housemates has their parents staying for the night or you will have to take the walk of shame in the morning.

You may find it hilarious to come in early in the morning drunk and noisy but someone else may have an exam or deadline the next morning.

4. Don't let irritation get out of hand

Living with people who are not your family can be a huge adjustment. They may have got used to very different ways of conducting daily life. If something bothers you, or is done in a manner you don't care for, have a chat; do not start an argument by tiptoeing around the incident. There is nothing more tiresome, for example, than an escalating war conducted through Post-it notes on the fridge. Have a chat if something grinds your gears (isn't that a marvellous expression?). You might save a fair amount of trees in the process too.

5. Don't hold a party and fail to include or inform housemates or neighbours

It's just mean and anyway, if you're going to make a lot of noise you're better off having them on side.

6. Put some pants on

No one will appreciate your nudity in the house unless you look like Ryan Gosling or Kate Moss which is really unlikely.

7. Don't gossip about other housemates

This can lead to segregation and feelings being hurt. Consider – if someone is gossiping with you what are they saying behind your back?

8. Communal areas are for sharing

Don't stretch out on the sofa and then not move when others come in. Also, eating in the kitchen rather than your room is more social and you will get to know your housemates better.

9. Just a reminder about the pants

SHARING

Dealing with sharing arises no matter who you live with. Unless you live in a palace you will probably have to share quite a lot of things – the 'facilities', the television, maybe a computer or even a bedroom. From as early as the 1590s we get a sense of the word sharing meaning 'to divide one's own and give part to others'. I don't know what they shared in the 1590s. Madrigals, perhaps. However much or little you have, sharing is a nice habit for life. As Charlotte Brontë said, 'Happiness quite unshared can scarcely be called happiness; it has no taste.'

Parts of the house

As Cleopatra no doubt said to Anthony, I'll get to the bedroom later. In the meantime it's worth having a think about the other divisions in the house.

The kitchen

It's communal. You don't need me to explain this in great detail. Learning to fill the dishwasher or wash up is not complicated. Take your turn.

Share appliances thoughtfully. If you need to wash your clothes and someone has left their laundry in the washing machine, put their items in a bag or the washing basket rather than placing them on the floor or the table. Don't leave them having to wash their clothes again.

The living room

Again, not a private space. The clue is in the name. It's where you all live. (Of course, some people call it the 'lounge', which sounds more relaxed, while others hint at the terraced nature of their property by saying the 'front room'. There's also 'sitting room', 'drawing room' and 'parlour'. I think you can only use the latter when you have a deceased relative from the nineteenth century who needs laying out.) Whatever you call it, this is the room where you socialise with each other. Try and find some way to agree on how you might do that. Sharing the TV may mean occasionally having to watch Top Gear or even, heaven forbid, sport.

The bathroom

Clear the drain in the bathroom. It's probably disgusting but it's also highly likely to be something disgusting that came from you.

Consider all the parts of yourself you might leave behind to the distress or discomfort of others. Toenail clippings or hairs – long ones, short ones and the curly ones no one wants to see left behind.

The loo

Clean up after yourself. No one wants to see someone else's bowel movement leftovers. And be fair about the loo roll. If you use the last piece, get a fresh roll. If you find that you are the only person buying loo roll for the house (as it runs out quickly) leave a note or tell someone that you are running low. Give everyone fair warning (preferably before they sit down …). Maybe leave an empty loo roll on the closed seat?

The garden

I once found a Victorian gardening book which contained the sentence 'No matter how small your garden do try to devote a couple of acres to wild flowers.' Sadly, such gardens are today on the rare side. Many gardens are small and, annoyingly, next to other people's gardens. This is worth bearing in mind if you decide to have a boisterous barbecue. Remember that your neighbours may not want to share the smoke from your fire or the beat of your music. It's also worth considering how much you want fast-growing conifers to establish your boundary if they also block someone else's light or view. Kindness. Sharing. And you never know when you might need a favour.

PREVENTING PROBLEMS

Household meeting

The worst families are those in which the members never really speak their minds to one another; they maintain an atmosphere of unreality, and every one always lives in an atmosphere of suppressed ill-feeling. It is the same with nations …

Introduction to second edition of *The English Constitution*
Walter Bagehot (1826–77)

Being part of a family or a shared household is a bit like being involved in running a tiny country. In our house I used to tell the kids they had been born into a dictatorship but luckily for them it was a benign one. Mary, you know that I am very interested in your opinions but that doesn't mean I will always agree to act on them. You're eight and I'm … well, I'm not. With my family we used to check the temperature of all members of the household with a quick meeting. These are especially useful with teenagers who sometimes believe that no one listens to them and that everyone is hateful. Pre-empting a teenage rebellion is always better than finding yourself behind the barricades whistling hits from *Les Misérables*.

Having a regular look at how everyone is doing with the house rules helps those who live together to carry on thinking it's a good idea. (In a household of flatmates these get-togethers can be more fun if held in a pub.)

1. Set a specific time for the meeting

Maybe sit up to table. Make it fun. Have some nice snacks.

2. Focus on the meeting

Turn off phones, televisions etc.

3. Take turns being in charge

It's nice to take even the youngest member seriously. They may surprise you with the way they run the meeting.

4. Make sure everyone has a say

If you're the parent and don't agree with the kids then explain why. If you're in a house-share remember some people are shy even if the extroverts find that annoying.

Home sweet home

The great Australian opera singer Dame Nellie Melba was very fond of singing 'Home, Sweet Home' as an encore. In fact you can hear a recording of it on YouTube. During the First World War she toured the United States playing Desdemona in Verdi's *Otello*. Her death scene was apparently magnificent and if the audience went wild enough, Dame Nellie used to get up, indicate for a piano to be wheeled to the stage whereupon she would sit down and accompany herself while singing 'Home, Sweet Home'. Once the applause had died down, she would once more collapse onto her deathbed and let poor Otello bring the whole thing to an end.

5. Check on everyone

Go round the table and find out what everyone is up to. I had three kids and a busy career. It can be hard to remember everything.

6. Finish on a positive note

Personally I think this is a good time for more snacks.

Make time for each other

Everyone seems so busy these days that even meals must be purchased ready-made to be nuked in a microwave. Take the time to prepare a meal for each other and to eat it at the table. It's the best way to keep in touch with each other and not suddenly be surprised at a turn in the life of someone who you ought to know well. My kids and I used to call it 'The Trough and Candle'. We would make dinner, light the candles and sit down together trying to come up with a piece of information that one of us knew which the rest of the table didn't. Some of it was most surprising.

OVERNIGHT GUESTS

Occasionally (and sometimes maddeningly) people who don't usually live with you will want to come and stay. This may mean having people inside your home circle who you would have preferred had stayed out. As neither the guest nor the host are used to living together it is a good idea to have some basic rules.

Rules for the host

Unbidden guests Are often welcomest when they are gone.

William Shakespeare (1564–1616)

1. Make your guest welcome

Even if you don't have a spare room, try to create a nice space for your guest to sleep. This may just be on the sofa but show that you have planned the sleeping arrangements before they turn up. If their stay is completely unexpected, such as someone missing the last bus and wishing to 'crash' on your sofa, still try to make it seem no trouble. Do your best to offer fresh bed linen, see if you can sort a bedside lamp and check they have all necessary toiletries. Having spare new toothbrushes is a good plan. There is a limit to what you may wish to share with even the most welcome visitor. It may be bad enough that they are staying at all – you don't want them having bad breath in the morning as well. Freeing up a drawer for them to put things in is nice but may encourage too long a stay.

2. Offer refreshments

Offer a drink as soon as they arrive and then show them where they can make one themselves. Even people of an excitable nature if they are British can be calmed by being able to make tea at will.

3. Be clear

Let your guests know what plans you have whilst they are staying with you. Do you have to work? Go to college? Attend a Star Trek convention? If you can't devote yourself full time to their care let them know. If you have to go to bed at a particular time, say so. Don't just yawn and hope they will take the hint – but hopefully they will.

Getting rid of galling guests

Getting rid of guests who don't take the hint is not easy. Being direct is always best but can cause trouble. The easiest method is, with regret, to stop being such a good host. Don't make such a fuss of meals, ask them to help with clearing up and so on. Finally, ask them what their plans are as you need to organise your timetable.

According to Elizabeth Burton in her book on Elizabethan England, hosts whose guests overstayed their sixteenth-century welcome used to play tricks on them. This included putting powdered vitriol and gall on a wet napkin which when used stained their skin black. This seems a little extreme – not to mention the tricky part of finding vitriol and gall.

Rules for the guest

No callers should fiddle with books, pictures, albums,
window-blinds, etc.

Collier's *Cyclopaedia of Social and Commercial Information*, 1882

1. Let the host know you're coming

Just because you met someone on a cruise or hitch-hiking across Australia, had a few drinks together and promised to stay friends forever doesn't mean they don't need a little notice that you are going to pitch up.

2. Be thoughtful

Bring a gift when you arrive and if you are staying for a little while notice things which are being used on a daily basis. Perhaps the host likes a particular brand of coffee which you could replace when it runs out. Be especially thoughtful about ...

3. Privacy

All the rules which apply to privacy in your own home should be especially highlighted when you stay with someone else. There are thresholds which you shouldn't cross. Some of them are literal – don't go into the host's bedroom unless specifically invited; some are metaphorical – don't delve into their private concerns unless specifically invited.

4. Don't treat the place like a hotel

Because it isn't one. Try to fit in with the general household arrangements. You cannot dictate meal times or bedtimes. If you don't like how the household is run there are places called 'hotels' which are always very clearly signposted.

5. You break it, you replace it

Simply apologise. Do not go on about it but make every effort to replace the item.

6. Don't overstay your welcome

It was the great American statesman, Benjamin Franklin, who said 'Guests, like fish, begin to smell after three days.' He was right. When Charles Dickens invited the Danish story-teller Hans Christian Andersen to stay at his Kent home, Gad's Hill, for two weeks in the summer of 1857 he didn't know it would ruin the friendship. Hans overstayed his welcome by three weeks, during which time he drove the family nuts. Dickens dropped subtle hints about Hans leaving and when he finally departed wrote on the mirror in the guest room – 'Hans Andersen slept in this room for five weeks – which seemed to the family AGES!' After that Dickens even stopped writing to his one-time Scandinavian friend. Oh dear, a story about a Dane behaving badly.

NEIGHBOURS

I love you, Brad. Brad! Brad! Look out! The shark's coming!

> Australian actress Natalie Imbruglia's favourite line from her time as Beth Brennan in the popular Australian soap *Neighbours*.

You can't choose your family or your neighbours so on the whole it's better, if possible, to just get on with what you've been given.

1. Be respectful

People who live next door come in a range of types, with at one end Hitler, who behaved so badly to his neighbour Poland, and at the other Aunt Fanny from the *Famous Five*, who always seemed so generous with her lashings of ginger beer. Most likely your own neighbours are people a bit like you. After all they live in rather similar accommodation. So think of what might annoy you – extraneous noise, rubbish, poor parking, bagpipe practice that kind of thing – and don't do it.

2. Be kind

Keep an eye on your fellow residents but not in a curtain twitching sort of way. No one wants to be the person who has to say 'I had no idea the man next door had been dead for three years.' Pop round and see if older locals are OK. Being neighbourly is actually rather pleasant and better than living on a border with barbed wire.

3. Keep them in the loop

Let your neighbours know if you are either having a massive party or digging a bunker. Both building works and entertainment can annoy.

4. Beware borrowing

Sugar is fine, even hedge cutters, but make sure things are returned or trouble can simmer and explode. My father used to have bookplates which read 'Never lend a book. Remember how you started your own library.'

5. Stay away from the solicitors

Once you go down the legal road you will never be at peace again. If there is a dispute – try to sort things if you can. It's not the Middle East. If it is the Middle East then you may be beyond my help.

THE STUDENT RETURNING HOME

I have never let my schooling interfere with my education.

Mark Twain (1835–1910)

I promise you, Mary, that starting out on your own is exciting. It is a time when you begin to think about how you want to live. Personally I have never recovered from the joy of eating ice cream for supper if I feel like it. If you do it right, being a grown-up is just like being a kid but with credit cards and without people telling you off. But however exciting it is out there, in theory nothing beats coming home. If you've been away you may now feel quite the adult. You may feel you have changed. Be aware that you may not be the only one. Your family may have got used to using your room for something else. For everyone, you included, adapting to having you back may not be easy.

1. Show how grown-up you are

Now you know how much it takes to run a place, help out a little. Offer to cook the family dinner – show off the recipes you have learned to cook by yourself. Behave like a grown-up and everyone will be so delighted they may let you carry on.

2. Keep your independence

You have been getting around university or college by yourself, so see if you can't still manage. Your folks are much more likely to be impressed and offer to give you a lift.

3. Do remember you are home now

It is great to come in at 4 a.m. in the morning, loud and boisterous from a night out, but maybe others in the house have work in the morning. Give them a break.

4. Do try to earn some money

Bear in mind how many years it's taken your parents to bring you up. They are tired now.

Parents of students returning home

1. Be enthusiastic about tattoos

It makes them seem less attractive to the young if old people think they are great.

2. Don't worry about your child's new partner

They are unlikely to stay the course but be polite to them in case they do.

3. Smile when you are patronised

You have to understand that the graduating student now knows everything there is to know and feels sorry for you. Be relieved that you no longer need to be clever.

Mary, home ought to be the place we all like best whoever we chose to share it with. It should be the place we recognise as being our little corner of the world. There is a lovely story about the composer Sir Arthur Sullivan. He was born in Bolwell Terrace off the Lambeth Walk in London. It is reported that he was returning home one night slightly the worse for wear from a party and was too befuddled to work out which was his home. He was, however, a brilliant musician, so he walked along kicking the metal foot scrapers at the base of the railings until he heard one that seemed familiar. 'That's it! E-flat,' he muttered, and went inside.

Hopefully we learn good behaviour in the comfort of our own homes and take it with us out into the wider world. There is an old expression that a person may be 'An angel in the street but a devil in the house'. That's not kind to anyone. Let's enjoy the time we spend with our loved ones. The Danes use the expression *'hygge'* which means to relax with loved ones, often over a meal or a drink. How nice – although it does bring us to some of the lengthiest lists of manners ever devised. Take a deep breath and join me at the table.

Much love

Sandi

2: TABLE MANNERS: EATING IN

Mata més gent la taula que la guerra.
(The table kills more people than war does.)

Catalan proverb from *Catalan Cuisine,* by Colman Andrews

Dear Mary

Are you ready? Because there seem to more rules about eating than almost anything else. It's not really surprising. No matter who you are or where you live, everyone has to eat. It is an activity no one can overlook and the development of cooking was important in the evolution of humans. Cooked food gives you more calories than raw. We don't know exactly when cooking started but it was probably first over an open fire and then later in a communal pot. As the food had to be shared, no doubt even cave dwellers had rules. After a hunt, the Inuit people of the Arctic always allow the men to eat first and then the women and children. This is not sexist. The men are the ones who've been out hunting. They are the coldest and hungriest in the group.

Some of the earliest manuscripts in the world have sections on dining etiquette. The fact is that table manners have been around for as long as there have been tables and these are probably the kind of guidelines I have bored you with most in our time together. Apart from early instructions not to bite others, table manners are the area of behaviour where parents often commence the civilising of their children. If parents weren't telling their kids to sit up straight and not speak with their mouth full then they were sitting at the table writing instructions about it.

Eating together is an important part of our lives. Who we share our food with helps give us a sense of community. The remarkable thing about a lot of the rules is how similar they actually are around the world. Mostly people of all types like it to be clean whenever and wherever they eat, and for the people they eat with to have consideration for them. Anyone who has sat through a family meal may have had a passing thought that they might not have chosen to be sitting there if they didn't all share some DNA.

TABLE MANNERS

Wherever you eat, table manners exist for three simple reasons:

1. Hygiene

This is very important. Let's not forget that Lucius Fabius Cilo, a Roman senator of the second century, died by choking to death on '… a single hair in a draught of milk'.

2. To stop us killing each other

Many people have rows at the dinner table but hardly anyone ever dies even though we generally sit quite close together with sharp objects in our hands. This is thanks to dining etiquette.

3. To stop us being greedy

The word *companion* comes from the Latin and means 'person with whom we share bread'. There are rules about eating, partly to ensure that everyone gets enough. The caveman slipped the bonds of bestial behaviour when he first uttered the words 'I've got bison. Does anyone want a bit?' and his partner replied, 'I've some berries that could go with that'. They sat down and no doubt the first eating rules arose to make sure everyone got a fair share. I also suspect the caveman had good manners about food because the good stuff used to be difficult to get hold of. It was treated with some respect. Go to a 'Food Court' in a shopping mall today where there is no shortage of anything and you may see the harm that plenty can do for manners.

Bad table manners

One of the worst things you can say about somebody is that they are not a pleasure to eat with. When David Bret wrote a biography of Rudolph Valentino, once widely believed to be the world's greatest lover, he tried to shock fans by suggesting that Valentino might have been a poor table companion. Bret claimed that one night when Valentino was dining with the writer, Elinor Glyn, and the movie producer, Jesse Lasky, Rudolph 'burped his way through five courses, ate all the leftovers from Lasky's and Glyn's plates, drank gravy from his own, and picked his nose with his teaspoon'. This is not the behaviour of someone at whom you want to make bedroom eyes.

In *The Old Curiosity Shop*, written in 1840, Charles Dickens confirmed the evil of the moneylender, Daniel Quilp, by giving him horrible table manners.

> ... he ate hard eggs, shell and all, devoured gigantic prawns with the heads and tails on, chewed tobacco and water-cresses at the same time and with extraordinary greediness, drank boiling tea without winking, bit his fork and spoon till they bent again, and in short performed so many horrifying and uncommon acts that the women were nearly frightened out of their wits, and began to doubt if he were really a human creature.

From such a description alone any reader might predict that life for Mr Quilp is not going to go smoothly. No doubt he would have had to be reminded about ...

Washing your hands

It's a good idea. If the washing is communal there are a few universal rules:

- Don't splash.
- Leave a bit of the towel dry for the next person.

Bog-standard rules about eating that everyone should know

1. Don't say 'bog' at the table

No one whilst eating likes to think about other bodily functions. Society has always worried about pollution, about catching things from each other, so we have strict rules to avoid contamination. Some of them are deeply engrained. Thus even a brand-new, never used loo brush could not be used to stir the soup. No one with a mouthful of food wants to think about the physical chain of events that is being set in motion. A number of cultures have strict rules about only using the right hand when eating or receiving food. This is because the left hand is considered 'unclean' as it is the hand used for 'hygienic' tasks.

While we are keeping clean …

2. Don't put your elbows on the table

I grew up in America where I was taught the old saying,

> Mabel, Mabel, strong and able, keep your elbows off the table, this is not a horse's stable, but a fancy dining table.

Not putting your elbows on the table is a very old chestnut and I hear you cry, 'Why can't I put my elbows where I like?' The simple answer is that there is a limited amount of space at a table and it needs to be shared. If you put your elbow on the table you may well stick it in someone else's dinner. This may have been more important in medieval times when people sat packed on long benches but even at a spacious dinner table it's still nice to remember that you are having a communal experience.

And while you're busy being communal it's also nice to look as though you are as interested in the company as in the food. If you sit hunched over your dinner with your elbows propping you up you look as though you're exhausted, with only a fascination for food keeping you upright. If you don't want to worry about others then consider that slouching also bends your spine and does your digestive system no favours at all. Eating with your elbows on the table is a great way to get indigestion. By all means put your elbows on the table when everyone has finished eating. By then the atmosphere is more relaxed. Some people loll back on their chairs and there is generally more room.

Finally, the 'no elbow' rule also has a hygiene aspect, with a general notion that one should keep unnecessary body parts off the table. Everyone wants to keep the eating surface as clean as possible. Who knows how clean your elbows might be? (Do I even need to say 'No feet on the table?' Surely not. If no one wants to see your elbow then they certainly won't be keen on your feet. They are the frayed edges of the body and in contact with the ground, so please keep your shoes on.)

The basic rule is that the only joint on the table during a meal should be one for carving. If you are a child who objects to this rule then think about the children of early American settlers. They weren't even allowed to sit at the table. They stood behind the grown-ups and ate whatever was passed to them.

3. Don't start before everyone has been served

It's a communal business in which we all look after each other. It is not a race. You are not starving. If you think you are starving leave immediately for any part of the developing world and have a rethink.

The exception is if the host or the person who has made the meal encourages people to begin to stop the meal getting cold. Once you have started don't just reach for things you want. You know why, don't you? Personal space. I think you're beginning to get the hang of this. It's all part of restraining the greed monster within us which has existed since the first stomach rumbled. Even Confucius, who lived back in 551–479 BC, wrote 'Do not snatch (at what you want)' when he covered table manners in his *Book of Rites*.

Finally, if you need a practical reason – you might knock something over with your arm.

4. Sit up and make an effort

If you slouch over your food or sit with your feet tucked under you, you seem less than engaged with everyone else at the table. The principal reason you should sit up is so you don't invade your neighbours' space. The age-old rule of not tipping your chair back on two legs is just common sense. You could fall. I once had a disastrous date with a young man (this is a very long time ago). We were eating in a restaurant which was divided into separate eating booths for each dining party. He tipped his chair back and crashed right through the divide into the next table of diners. It was not a successful evening.

It's nice for everyone if you generally look presentable. No matter how hot it is, never sit at the table without a shirt on (unless, of course, given special permission by the King of Denmark). There are very few people whose physiques are so perfect that other people want to look at them while trying to swallow.

5. Chew with your mouth closed

Again we're dwelling in the unsavoury land of other's moistness. Mastication, like another similar word, is a private affair. According to an Elizabethan book of manners published in 1577 (*A New Yeeres Gift: The Courte of Civill Courtesie*), if you open your mouth while eating, people will see 'the food rowle by – which is a foule sight and loathsome' and I don't suppose much has changed over the years. Avoiding others having to look at food 'rowling by' is also the reason why one shouldn't speak with one's mouth full. If you have something to say wait till your mouth is empty. Rare is the person who has such a conversational gem that it won't wait till they've swallowed.

Associated with keeping the mouth closed is anything to do with the tongue. Licking of all sorts is to be discouraged – fingers, lips, cutlery, etc. On the whole the tongue belongs inside the mouth. Think how rude it is to stick it out at someone.

There are other add ons to this rule:

- Don't overfill your mouth.

- Don't gobble. In fact just generally don't make funny noises when you eat or drink.

- Do I need to add 'Don't slobber' to this list? I think not.

6. Don't pick your teeth

If we don't want to look at food being masticated in your mouth then we certainly don't want to dwell on the bits that got stuck on the way down. If you get something caught in your teeth try to leave it until you can excuse yourself from the table. If it is terrible then excuse yourself from the table. Toothpicks should be used in private. If you can't leave the table and you absolutely have to remove something then bring your napkin up to cover your mouth while ejecting the offending item.

While we're on grooming, there are a few other matters:

- Don't play with your hair, and never comb it. It will get in someone else's food. Remember the dead Roman with the hairy milk?

- Don't put on make-up at the table. Your grooming regime works best if it's a secret.

7. Don't pick your nose

Clearly the whole nose thing has been an ongoing table problem. In the thirteenth century a German poet and musician called Tannhäuser wrote a poem called *Hofzucht* (Court Behaviour) in which he spent a lot of time telling people not to blow their noses into their hands. It's not the usual stuff of verse-making but then he also managed to find rhymes to stop people putting chewed bones back into the communal bowl or sticking their fingers in the mustard.

Erasmus, in his kid's manners tome, declared 'Do not blow your nose with the same hand that you use to hold the meat' and you can see his point. On the whole human beings have never liked other people's moistness. I'm talking about the great S's our bodies produce – spit, sweat, snot, shit and I'm sure you can think of others you wouldn't want to come up at the table. It's a rare person who likes someone else's slimy output. About the only body excretion we can cope with is tears because they seem fairly pure, but even they can become tiresome. If you have a cold or think you may want to blow your nose, bring a handkerchief or tissue to the table. Do not sniff.

Never blow your nose on your napkin. Someone else is likely to have to clear it and won't want to deal with your effluence. If you have used your paper napkin by mistake to blow your nose DO NOT put it crumpled up back on the table or even your plate. Keep it with you until you can dispose of it.

I could add 'don't use the tablecloth either' but I like to think we can presume there is a baseline of basic manners on which to build.

8. Avoid all expellations of wind

For most diners the coughing, sneezing, belching, farting etc. of other diners is not welcome. If you feel a cough or sneeze coming, turn your head away from the table and cover your mouth.

No one likes other people's flatulence and, in truth, very few are keen on their own. If you feel windy at a work event it is worth considering the possible consequences. In 2003 there was an IT fellow called Goran Andervass who worked for the Swedish national bank, Riksbanken. Early one morning a colleague came into Goran's office and let rip some wind. Goran was furious and began shouting. Goran must have carried on being cross because eventually he was discharged from the bank. He sued and won 850,000 kronor compensation (about £65,000). 'If a fart is done on purpose when going into somebody's office,' the Swedish Work Environment Authority declared, 'it is important that management takes the matter seriously.'

In this windy category we can add 'Don't blow on your food'. It seems simple – if your food is too hot to touch then it will be too hot to eat. Wait a bit. Restraint. We're not Neanderthals, remember? Don't blow a mistral of bad breath over the table in an effort to cool your meal.

9. Use your napkin

Napkins exist to get rid of unwanted mess and moisture. They are an essential part of eating without annoying and have been for about 3,000 years. The first sort of napkin was a dough mixture used by the Spartans. It was called *apomagdalie* and it was kneaded at the table after a meal to clean the hands. The ancient Romans were the first to move on to cloth, with guests bringing to meals their own *mappae*, a fairly large sheet of material, to avoid toga and couch staining. Napkins used to be huge but then, according to the poet Ben Jonson, 'Forks arrived in England from Italy "to the saving of napkins".'

Today napkins are often fairly small squares of paper. Put yours out of sight on your lap. If you get food on your lips, use the napkin to dab them. If you have to leave the table unexpectedly, put your napkin on your chair. No one wants to look at it. At the end of the meal place the napkin either on or beside your plate.

10. General noise

Eating should not be a noisy occupation and that includes the consuming of soup. Eat it quietly, tipping the bowl away from you and using the side of the spoon.

Don't play games while eating. That includes mucking about with the cutlery, plates, sugar, moulding your bread into chess pieces and so on. Focus, people, focus.

11. Never use your phone at the table

Back to the communal part of eating. Focus on the people you are sharing a meal with, not someone who isn't even in the room. Don't put your phone on the table as if you're hoping to be interrupted by something more important. If you do get a call and it relates to an emergency – excuse yourself, get up and go to another room.

- Do not text your friends.

- Do not tweet about your meal. It's dull for everyone including those people who have been foolish enough to 'follow' you.

- Be in the moment. If someone is using their phone incessantly at the table you could text them and say that there is something important that requires their attention, i.e. you.

12. Don't make love at the table

It's wonderful to be in love but people will not want to hear the noises of you kissing which are reminiscent of poor plumbing.

Gosh that was a lot of Don'ts. Here are a couple of Dos:

- Do enjoy the time at the table with your family and friends. We lead fragile lives of indeterminate length and never know how much time we all have together. I would give almost anything to have another meal with my departed father.

- Do enjoy your food. Take your time. Years ago I entered Mozambique a few weeks after the conclusion of the civil war. A street market had sprung up, selling a few basics. The people were poorer than any European could ever imagine and I was amazed to see garlic for sale. 'Why would you spend money on garlic if you are so poor?' I asked my guide. She turned and took me by the shoulders, shaking her head, 'Sandi, we are poor not dead. We still want our food to taste nice.'

Reigning cats and dogs

There is more on pets later but here is an early and shocking assertion for animal lovers – not everyone is as keen on our four-legged friends as they are. Medieval manners books asked children not to 'stroke or cat or dog' while eating and nothing much has changed. Again it's to do with cleanliness, so don't encourage a creature which may shed its hair to lounge about under the table, and certainly don't feed it. It takes genuine passion for a pet to enjoy the sound of it salivating.

I once belonged to a club for women graduates. I asked them if they had any specific rules for the dining room which I needed to know. 'Only one', replied the chairwoman. 'We do have a "no goat rule".' As we were in central London I naturally enquired further and it transpired that a country member had always brought her goat with her but it 'made such a mess of the dining room curtains that in the end, with regret, we had to bring in a rule.'

CUTLERY

Forks

The custom of the priests with the people was that when any man offered sacrifice, the priest's servant would come, while the meat was boiling, with a three-pronged fork in his hand …

The Bible, English Standard Version, I Samuel 2:13

The word fork comes from the Latin *furca* or 'pitchfork'. It consists of two parts – the prongs which are called 'tines' and the handle known as the 'shaft'. The general European rule is to keep the tines down unless it is the only cutlery you are using in which case you can scoop with them up. Americans are happy to scoop up at any time.

Some forking history

The *fork* was invented because some things when cooked are too hot to hold. This has never changed. The ancient Egyptians used large forks for cooking, as did the Greeks, and there were bone forks found in Chinese burial sites from more than 4,000 years ago. Frankly, forks are now a perfect pest in museums.

The idea of having your own fork probably started with the Romans during the Byzantine period. So somewhere between 330–1453, which gives quite a lot of scope for error. (To be honest it could just as easily have been the Greeks, but believe me, it was a long time ago.) Before then people lifted a bowl or plate to the mouth rather than use an implement. The transition to using the fork for eating rather than just serving starts in the mid fifteenth century when posh people decided they no longer wanted to touch their food.

Thomas Coryat (c.1577–1617)

If you live in the UK and have a rather random fork loathing, then Coryat is the man to blame. Having spent a little time at court as a sort of jester, he set off tramping about Europe and parts of Asia in an Elizabethan/Jacobean version of an extended gap year. He wrote celebrated books about his travels, including *Coryat's Crudities hastily gobbled up in Five Months Travels in France, Italy, &c.* (1611). From Italy he brought back descriptions of two things which would change English life forever. One was the 'umbrella' and the other was the table fork. The UK was one of the last European countries to adopt the fork, as their use was seen by some as 'effeminate and affected'. No one was all that keen on the umbrella either. Coryat died of dysentery while travelling in Surat in 1617. Might have been something he'd eaten.

In the tenth century we know that the fork was all over the parts of the world we now think of as the Middle East and Turkey. Royalty spread the word. It was Catherine de' Medici who brought forks to France and the Infanta Beatrice, mother of King Manuel I, who introduced them to Portugal. By 1600 wealthy Italians were carrying their own fork and spoon in a box called a *cadena*. In Perrault's original fairy tale of *Sleeping Beauty* (*La Belle au bois dormant*, 1697), each of the fairies invited for the christening is given a 'fork holder' as a memento.

It took the British rather longer to take to the fork and the Americans longer still. In 1630, Governor Winthrop of the Massachusetts Bay Colony in the fledgling America, owned the first and only fork which he is said to have demonstrated to his people on 25 June. Many thought it an insult to God. As late as the nineteenth century, American forks were still sometimes referred to as 'split spoons'.

Knives

De flesta självmord begås med kniv och gaffel.
(Most suicides are committed with a knife and fork.)

Swedish proverb

I was taught at boarding school never to use a knife while dining unless it was absolutely essential. Sadly, nothing we ever ate at school required the presence of a knife. I am left with the bizarre skill of being able to spear, divide and consume a whole Scotch egg using only a fork. Potatoes, vegetables, omelettes, shepherd's pie – all were divided and eaten with the edge of a fork. As a consequence I remain a devoted fan of the knife and its correct use.

Knife work if you can get it

There was a time when everyone carried their own knife. It was sharp and pointed and for centuries hosts tried to stop guests picking their teeth with it after a meal. People were rather particular about their knives and, a bit like toothbrushes, didn't like sharing.

The dinner knife, a much less threatening implement with a rounded tip, is said to have been invented on 13 May 1637 which, if you like your cutlery history carved up precisely, is quite pleasing. Bizarrely, it was invented by the First Minister of France, Cardinal Richelieu. You'd think he had better things to do, but apparently one night at a formal dinner he saw a guest picking his teeth with a sharp knife and had had enough. He ordered all his knives ground down and rounded off to stop such disgusting behaviour. In 1669 King Louis XIV made it illegal for French cutlers to forge pointed dinner knives.

Before stainless steel was invented in the early twentieth century, knives were all made of steel which was said to affect the taste of fish and fruit. This meant that those who could afford them had separate knives made of silver for fruit which did not react to the acid in the fruit. For similar reasons fish knives were also made of silver, although up until the 1880s most people ate fish using two forks to separate the flesh from the bone. The bizarre shape of fish knives was all part of Victorian innovation and not really necessary. By the late twentieth century fish knives were seen as very middle class, and they are on the pointless side.

There are some very basic rules about knives, most of which relate to safety:

1. Don't sit with your knife in the air

You could have someone's eye out.

2. Don't point with your knife

The eye again.

3. Don't eat from your knife

The most fundamental rule is that this is not a suitable implement to convey food to your mouth for the simple reason that you could cut your tongue. The blood vessels in the tongue bleed profusely and can spurt – this never goes well at either your own or someone else's table.

4. Mind yourself

Hold the knife in your right hand with the index finger extended over the top of the blade to keep it steady when you are cutting.

American v. European cutlery use – hidden handle v. zig-zag

Europeans keep their knife in the right hand and their fork in the left. Americans favour what is known as 'zig-zag' eating. They hold the knife in the right and the fork in the left to cut their meat. Then they transfer the fork to the right hand to bring the food to their mouth. Neither method is 'wrong' although the European method is seen as more efficient. If you wish to draw the least attention to your eating as possible then probably the European method causes the least fuss.

Spoons

دینکن فرصم قشاق کی زا رتش کی

A camel does not drink from a spoon.

Persian Proverb

That is so true yet you rarely see it written down.

The spoon has been around since Palaeolithic times. Basically spoons are really old. The great aunt in the cutlery canteen. Before some genius invented the spoon there is no doubt people used shells to scoop food up if it was too hot to touch. The word spoon comes from Old Norse *sponn* meaning 'chip or splinter' so some people probably used a bit of wood. After that you find the ancient Egyptians using spoons, the usual catalogue of Greeks and Romans, ancient Indians and Muslims etc. Everyone thought the spoon was a cracking idea.

Pasta

Those who forget the pasta are condemned to reheat it.

Anon.

It may thrill the child in you to know that pasta was originally eaten with the hands. The first pasta factory opened in Venice in 1740 and illustrations from the time show Venetians tilting their heads back and dangling spaghetti in. It was the addition of sauce in later years which made this tricky and introduced the fork. When eating out it is considered poor form to cut spaghetti up. This is a rare instance of eating with a fork and spoon. Place the fork in the right hand, pick up some spaghetti on the tines, place the end of the tines against the bowl of the spoon and twirl the pasta onto the fork before placing it in the mouth. This requires a little practice but is well worth it for the savings you will make at the dry-cleaners.

Chopsticks

Man who catch fly with chopstick capable of anything.

Mr Miyagi, *The Karate Kid*

The English word 'chopstick' may have derived from Chinese pidgin English, in which 'chop chop' meant 'quickly'. The Japanese call them *hashi* meaning 'bridge' as they are the means to get the food from the bowl to the mouth. It is worth learning how to use them, as they are frequently presented in Asian restaurants which are all over the place. According to the National People's Council of China it takes 20 million mature trees a year to make the 80 billion pairs of disposable chopsticks needed annually by 1.4 billion Chinese people. The environmental cost may mean a move to cutlery.

While they are still around remember that there are many rules about chopsticks. The Japanese take chopstick use as seriously as we treat cutlery and they have many terms for poor stick handling, including *Saguri-hashi* – searching the bowl with your chopsticks to see if there is anything left that you want. The critical thing to remember is that it is rude to lick chopsticks. It's that old tongue thing again. No one wants to see it. The Japanese call licking chopsticks *neburi-hashi*. It's a definite no-no.

Eating with fingers

'... *it is difficult to believe that fingers once did duty as forks* ...'

Manners and Rules of Good Society by 'A Member of the Aristocracy', 1888

Notions about what constitutes good manners come and go in cycles. It's worth bearing in mind that for all his punctiliousness about etiquette, Louis XIV never used a fork in his life. When I was a child it was practically forbidden to eat anything with one's fingers. The only exception seemed to be 'things that could fly'. Thus one could pick up a chicken wing but not a lamb chop. I have no idea why this exception was thought of and no one else seems to either.

Before the invention of cutlery people had no choice but to eat with their fingers. When the ancient Romans and Greeks sat down for a meal they didn't. Sit, that is. They lay on their sides with their heads pointing toward the table. One hand propped them up while the other reached for the food.

Gradually the idea developed in the West that it was some mark of civilisation not to touch our food. Even today we can be fairly confident that, if the dinner is described as 'finger-lickin' good' it is probably not going to be the most formal affair. Today a lot of food is provided that can be eaten without cutlery. One reason to avoid 'finger food' is that most if it is not very healthy – chips, pizza, chicken nuggets, etc. Even if it's acceptable to use your fingers, there are still a few rules that help make the meal a little more pleasant for everyone.

1. It's not a race

Put the food down between bites. Just because it's 'fast food' doesn't mean you have to hoover it up.

2. Take small bites

This will stop fillings such as ketchup shooting out of the meal.

3. Use your napkin

4. There is no anti-cutlery rule

Even if everyone else is using their hands you can use a knife and fork if you prefer. In February 2013, a branch of the hamburger chain McDonalds in the seaside suburb of Warilla, south of Sydney, became the first in the world to offer customers the option of plates, cutlery and table service.

Eating peas

The chapter of peas is still continuing; the impatience waiting to eat them, the pleasure of having eaten them and the joy of eating more are the three points our princes have been making for four days... it's a fad, it's a craze.

Madame de Maintenon,
Mistress and then wife to Louis XIV, 1635–1719

You're probably wondering – what was the biggest day in pea history? Well, I am here to serve. It was 18 January 1660. A hamper including peas in their shells from Genoa was presented to King Louis XIV of France. His aide, Count de Soissons, started shelling them for him and a food craze was born. Courtiers went mad for this luxury item, while in fairy tales princesses proved their credentials by being able to feel a single pea through many mattresses.

Peas are, however, a devil to eat because they are small, very mobile and too brilliantly coloured for anyone to overlook should they shoot off the plate. Handling them well takes practice. Ideally you should hold the fork tines down and try to crush the verdant devils onto the points. The fork shouldn't be turned into a scoop unless you are in America where it is more acceptable. The critical thing is not to fret about it. One of the easiest options is to use some potato or other soft food to help squash them on to the fork. Don't use your fingers or your spoon.

Picnics

When a picnic party is to proceed to its destination by rail, a saloon carriage is engaged beforehand …

Manners and Rules of Good Society
by 'A Member of the Aristocracy', 1888

Bizarrely, the meals where we allow ourselves to eat informally are usually the meals which require the most preparation. Much packaging of food is done, many miles are often travelled in order to lounge on a blanket and eat outdoors with stones in our shoes and grass in our hair. Eating with your fingers is fine here although napkins are still essential.

A quick aside about cannibalism

Is it progress if a cannibal uses a knife and fork?

Stanislaw Lem (1921–2006), Polish author

Every human society has some kind of eating rules. Even people who thought it was all right to eat visitors had no-go areas of behaviour. Back in 1502, when Montezuma took the throne to rule the Aztec empire, cannibalism was rife. People ate parts of the body according to their status, and no one would barbecue bodies without offering Montezuma one thigh from each corpse. (He liked them with tomatoes and chilli pepper sauce apparently.)

Barbecues

Again we're in the finger area. The whole meal is a social curiosity in which meat becomes an entirely masculine preserve. Men stride about with an apron on, like a slightly prissy man-the-hunter. Although if you are a woman, let them know that man the hunter is unlikely to become man-who-cleans-grill-pan-afterwards.

Iculanibokola

The iculanibokola is a specialist fork from Fiji which if your Fijian host put one on the table in the nineteenth century might have caused you to consider leaving. Up until the 1890s cannibalism was part of Fijian culture. It was believed that the power of an enemy could be taken if you ate him. It was, however, considered wrong for chiefs and priests to touch food with their hands. The use of this special fork removed that problem whilst also indicating the significance of the meal. Some iculanibokola were fancier than others. It was a great way to show off your status and get guests to go home.

Right, that covers the basics, but some meals take a bit more planning. These also often require your 'best bib and tucker'. I'm sure you know what a 'bib' is but perhaps a 'tucker' is more mysterious. It was a lace piece which a woman wore on her front from the seventeenth to the late nineteenth century to protect her modesty, by which time it must have been filthy. You don't need one now, but you will perhaps require a bit of sprucing up as we head off to think about something a bit more formal.

Much love

Sandi

3: TABLE MANNERS: DINING OUT

The world was my oyster but I used the wrong fork.

Oscar Wilde (1854–1900), Irish author

Dear Mary

Right. I think we are ready to widen our circle as we begin to include those with whom we don't share our daily lives. There are various settings for more formal dining. We'll start with when you want to impress someone in your own home, then pop into a restaurant before finishing up with the potentially more daunting banquet or celebratory meal.

DINNER PARTIES – BEING THE HOST

The very words 'Host' and 'Guest' can tell you a lot about the potential danger of a dinner party. They both derive from the Indo-European *ghostis* meaning stranger. It's also the original root for the word 'hostile'. Unless handled well a dinner party can be fraught with awkwardness. They can, however, also be a lovely way to spend time. The last thing Jesus is supposed to have done is gather his friends for supper. The important thing to remember is that all the usual rules of home dining apply plus a few extra.

How many guests?

The number of guests at dinner should not be less than the number of the Graces nor exceed that of the Muses, i.e., it should begin with three and stop at nine.

Marcus Terentius Varro (116–27 BC), Roman scholar

Thirteen used to be thought of as such an unlucky number at the dinner table. It is often suggested that this stems from Judas being the thirteenth person to sit down at the Last Supper, but this seems unlikely. The Bible tells us many things but overlooks the seating plan for that evening. Whatever its origins, *triskaidekaphobia* (fear of the number thirteen) was so common in nineteenth-century Paris that there were men called *quartorzième* which means 'fourteenth'. They would dress for dinner and then wait at home until they were sent for to make up the numbers at a dinner party where someone had dropped out and there was a danger of thirteen people sitting down at the table. Today you can find the superstition catered for at the Savoy Hotel in London where a metre-high sculpture of a black cat called Kaspar is available to make up the numbers at any table seating thirteen.

The number to invite today is shockingly simple – it depends how much room you have at your table. If you are of a mathematical bent then ideally you want to allow about half a metre for each guest's place setting. If you have a small table and want everyone to sit down then you need to invite fewer guests. Easy, isn't it? Eating a meal in cramped conditions is not fun.

Now, who to invite?

Geltungsbedürfnis

This wonderful German word translates as 'craving for recognition.' Some people have dinner parties as a sort of ego trip. They invite not their friends but a mix of people who they feel will show them in a good light. This is not always a success. Think about the mix of people and how they will get on rather than how they will reflect on your own status. I once attended a dinner which included the pop singer Geri Halliwell and the former White House intern,

Monica Lewinsky. I had a very engaging chat with Monica but she knew no one and spent the evening looking rather at sea. (Many people seemed anxious in her company. I don't know what they were worrying about – suddenly mentioning dry-cleaning or cigars, perhaps.) It's also worth bearing in mind that not everyone has the same ideas about who might impress. I failed to cover myself with glory when I spent forty-five minutes chatting to Ms Halliwell and then asked her what she did for a living.

(Side note – the German language is full of wonderful words. I don't think *Weltschmerz*: 'world-pain' or world-weariness can be improved in another language. My father told me that an early German word for tank was *Schutzengrabenvernichtungpanzerkraft-wagen*. Roughly translated I think it means trench-crossing vehicle used for destruction. Papa said they lost the First World War because it took so long to tell the tanks to move.)

Do invite

Your friends, of course, but also some people you don't know well but would like to. You never know, but you may not yet have met all the fabulous folk there are to encounter.

Don't invite

- People who will only talk shop.
- Other guests' exes.

Invitations

The way in which you invite people indicates how much you care about whether they come. It also says something about the importance of the event. Most weddings, for example, are not an impulse occasion so taking the time to write by hand shows the significance of both the occasion and that the presence of the guest matters to you. Email is fine for a more impromptu or informal event such as dinner with friends. Text is all right for your nearest and dearest but in general don't invite via a phone call as it makes it very difficult for people to refuse.

Make it easy for someone not to come. You don't want anyone there who wishes they weren't. Don't send invitations too early so that people can't get out of it and don't make them so open-ended that people feel trapped. My least favourite invitations to attend an event say something like 'Please come and speak on any day at all in the next five years'. This leaves you with no other option except to say, rather rudely, that you don't want to.

Make sure everyone knows they are invited for dinner and not just drinks. How hideous to shop and cook for someone who has already eaten.

Give people a chance to declare their dietary peculiarities. No tofu addict wants to attend a hog roast.

Be ready when the guests arrive

(It all seems so obvious when you write it down, doesn't it?) The reason you are having a dinner party is not just to have dinner. You may want to impress someone, develop a friendship or thank someone for a kindness. No one wants to be invited and find their host is in a panic so give yourself plenty of time to get all your preparation done. Making lists of everything you have to do beforehand is a good way to make sure you don't overlook something.

- Tidy up. No one wants to see your dirty clothes or your taste in niche interest magazines.

- Make sure the loo is clean and that there is soap and a fresh towel.

- Make sure there is loo paper.

- Don't have music so loud no one can speak. Remember that the older generation may not have such brilliant hearing but still want to be included. Hard as it is to believe, you will be old yourself one day.

- Turn the TV off. I didn't really have to put that, did I?

The food

If you are not confident about cooking and chatting at the same time serve something that can be pre-prepared and put in the oven. The guests have come to be with you, not sit by themselves in another room while you fret over the food.

If the meal goes wrong and is inedible – laugh and have a takeaway. These are your friends. If they are not your friends their reaction will help you decide if they might become friends. Whatever you do, try to make sure there is enough for everyone. There is another story about the director Alfred Hitchcock whose very profile showed a man keen on his food. One day he went to dinner at someone's house where he felt not enough food had been served. At the end of the evening, the host very politely said to the great man 'I do hope you will dine with us again soon.' 'By all means,' he replied. 'Let's start now.'

Make an effort

In the *Domus Aurea*, also known as the Golden House, according to the Roman historian, Suetonius (c. AD 69–122)

> All the dining rooms had ceilings of fretted ivory, the panels of which could slide back and let a rain of flowers, or of perfume from hidden sprinklers, fall on his guests.

This is beyond most people but it is perfectly possible to set a nice table. In medieval times this was hard work. No one had a full-time dining table. If people wanted to eat, boards had to be laid across trestles – literally 'laying the table'. I remember a wonderful meal in the studio of the Danish sculptor and painter, Robert Jacobsen, when I was a child. The entire touring company of the Royal Copenhagen Theatre had turned up unexpectedly, so great vats of spaghetti were laid out on an impromptu table made out of beer crates and old doors. I imagine students do something rather similar all the time.

'Setting the table'

Nowadays the basics are very straightforward:

* The fork goes on the left. It has four letters just like 'left'.

* The knife goes on the right. It has five letters just like …

anyway, make sure the sharp edge of the knife lies to the left, facing the plate. That way when someone picks it up they are less likely to cut themselves accidentally.

- The dessert spoon is placed above the dinner plate with handle pointing to the right. (If there is a dessert fork as well the handle of that points to the left.)

- A soup spoon has a wider bowl. It is placed on the extreme right of the plate.

- A silver spoon is usually found in a rich person's mouth.

- The English lay spoon bowls and fork tines facing up, while the French put them face down. North American owners of very old silver may use the French manner to show off the monograms on the backs of the cutlery.

- Be certain that everything is clean. Rubbing an old bit of dried egg off a plate before being served never helps heighten the enjoyment.

- If you have a centrepiece don't make it such a vast statement of artistic expression that your guests can't see each other.

The rest

It doesn't matter whether you have lots of nice matching china. I go to a wonderful restaurant in Canterbury that uses a hotchpotch of old china from charity shops and it looks great. This isn't about being rich, it's about making an effort.

The rule for candles is simple – use them when it's dark. Everyone looks better by candlelight but it mustn't be so dark that people start stabbing each other instead of the main course. Think about the lighting where you are serving the food. You need a glow not gloom. Candles are worth the effort. They suggest luxury as they are generally unnecessary.

Napkins are essential and a tablecloth is a nice touch. If you can't afford napkins even some nicely folded kitchen paper is better than nothing.

Seating plan

If you invite a mixed group of people to dinner, some of whom you don't know well, have a think in advance about where everyone is going to sit. It is the host's job to arrange the seating.

In the old days this was easy, as there was a very clear hierarchy of eating. History is littered with endless reports of medieval banquets where we have no idea what was eaten but we know where everyone sat. In those days salt was considered very valuable and was placed before the lord of the house and his family. Their table was often raised on a dais so people either sat 'below the salt' – or above it.

In his snappily entitled work on manners written in 1460, *The Boke of Nurture for Men, Seruauntes and Chyldren with Stans Puer Ad Mensam, Newly Corrected, Very Vtyle and Necessary Vnto All Youth*, John Russell spent a lot of time describing the endless rules for a seating plan. These days there is less to worry about.

In the UK the host usually takes the head of the table with their partner at the other end, while in France and other Latin countries sometimes the host sits in the middle of the long side. As for the guests, some of it is very basic – probably don't put the raging homophobe next to someone with a new civil partner, although it might be best, anyway, if they came to separate events.

There are elaborate rules about rank. For example, the lady of the highest rank sits on the host's right – but these are unlikely to trouble you. If you don't know them you probably don't need to.

When to serve dinner

The easy answer is 'when it's ready'. Different cultures have their own idea about how soon you eat after you arrive. In the West it is common to socialise for at least half an hour before the meal is served. It is a kindness for the host to consider the guests' own timetable. If it is a 'school night' serving dinner late is not kind. I once attended an evening where, two hours after we had arrived, the host declared brightly, 'I think I'll put the dinner on now'. The fact that he is still alive only highlights the astonishingly good manners of the guests.

Saying grace

This is less common today although you find the idea of saying thanks for sustenance in many cultures. Some thank a supreme being for making humans supreme over animals and plants and some thank the animals and plants themselves. If people were previously unaware that you are religious it may make them feel uncomfortable. That's not to say you shouldn't do it but it can cause a little frisson. Perhaps you can give a general thanks without making the atheist or non-believer feel they are heading straight for hell after or even during the meal.

Grace is still said at very formal meals. I am not religious and host a lunch every year where I am asked to say grace. I use that as a moment for the gathered diners to reflect and begin by saying:

> I am mindful that within this room there are representatives of every kind of faith as well as those who choose not to believe, but I think we can join together in the knowledge that there are some desires and needs which are universal. Let's not forget that the word 'Amen' is found in Christianity, Judaism and Islam and, for the atheist or agnostic, it is an expression that simply means 'So be it'. So let us close our eyes and join together in thought as we remember those less fortunate than ourselves.

There is a lovely story about the American journalist Bill D. Moyers who between 1965 and 1967 served as White House Press Secretary to President Lyndon Baines Johnson. One day Moyers was called upon to say grace at lunch. 'Speak up, Bill,' Johnson shouted. 'I can't hear a damn thing.' 'Mr President,' Moyers is said to have replied quietly, 'I wasn't addressing you.'

Drinks

'[The English] drink no water, unless at certain times upon religious score, or by way of doing penance'.

Sir John Fortescue, c. 1470

Most guests would expect to be provided with an alcoholic beverage to accompany a meal. If you have some reason for not wishing to serve alcohol in your house – religious, medical and so on – it's a good idea to let your guests know in advance so they know what to expect. If you do serve alcohol and a guest says that they would prefer a soft drink, do not attempt to change their mind. For all you know they may be recently released from rehab. (See separate section on alcohol in general.)

Making a toast to welcome everyone as they sit down is a nice touch.

Beginning the meal

The host should never start until everyone has been seated and served. You must have invited the guests for a reason, so check they are comfortable. Don't insist everyone tries everything. They are not children. They may have forgotten to mention their unusual reaction to Brussels sprouts.

During the meal

Keep an eye on everyone. See that they have what they need. Make sure everyone is being included in the conversation and head off any potential arguments by changing the subject. Dinner is a place of peace. One of the cornerstones of civility is noticing other people's needs, so be watchful to see how your guests are getting on and whether they require something. This does not mean overfilling people's plates. This may be your favourite meal but it might not suit everyone, so even if you think the food is marvellous try not to praise it yourself. If someone compliments you that's just nice.

Dessert

The serving of pudding usually alerts the guests that the dining drama is nearly over. The origin of the term dessert is from the French *desservie* meaning to de-serve or clear the table. Dessert was intended to clear the palate. In France the dessert may be served after the cheese. If you are not in France but are pretentious enough to follow this regime do let guests know so they don't fill up on cheese.

Coffee

The Turks have a beverage the colour of which is black. One swallows it hot, not only during the meal, but after.

Letter from Pietro della Valle, 7 February 1615

These days lots of people would like a hot drink after a meal but are worried that it might keep them awake. Provide a non-caffeine alternative if you don't want your guests ringing you at 2 a.m. for a chat.

Smoking

* Don't. It's bad for you.

* If you must then go outside.

* If you go outside don't leave cigarette ends. Hopefully you will have an excellent host who has provided a receptacle. I have a rather pleasing ashtray which makes the sound of a cough when you flick ash in it.

Entertainment

No one is as interested in your holiday pictures, photos from childhood or pics of your kids as you are. Do not be tempted into a full-length show, however much your guests seem interested. They are just being polite. If your guest brings out photo albums that they've brought with them, spend time planning your next party without them.

Do not bring out musical instruments, board games or fire up the PlayStation unless you know people very well indeed. What amuses you may not be for general consumption. Of course things can never be as bad as any dinner party with the Roman Emperor, Elagabalus, who was the world's worst host. He came to power in AD 218 when he was just fourteen. He makes Nero look positively sensible and only managed to last four years partly because no on could stand his manners. He is said to have invented a prototype for the whoopee-cushion; occasionally he would serve his poorer dinner guests with paintings of food so that they remained hungry; worst of all, he would get his guests drunk and then let lions, leopards, panthers and bears into their bedrooms while they slept off the effects. Even a guest who brought their own game of *Twister* with them today doesn't seem quite so bad.

Saying goodbye

It's not always easy to bring things to a conclusion but saying things along the lines of 'This has been such fun' is usually a good clue that it's time to wrap up. Don't let your guests clear up no matter how much they offer unless they are close family in which case they can help themselves. Take people to the door and make sure they have everything. Make an effort to ensure they have had a good time right to the end.

DINNER PARTIES – BEING THE GUEST

Refusing an invitation

The American author, William Faulkner, once declined an invitation to dinner at the White House with the words 'Why that's a hundred miles away. That's a long way to go just to eat.' We may not all have that kind of courage but everyone is entitled to turn down an invitation if they wish. Your time is your own but the worst thing is to give a lot of excuses. Saying 'That would have been lovely but I'm afraid I can't' or 'Maybe some other time' is sufficient. If the host insists on making another date then you need to think generally about your boundaries with people. If you are going to turn someone down, do it quickly so they can replace you with someone else.

Accepting an invitation

The basic rule is accept speedily and in the same manner as the invitation was extended. So if the invite was by email, reply in an email and so on.

Give your host plenty of notice if you have any particular dietary problems

It seems quite the fashion these days to have one kind of food allergy or another. Some of them can be very trying for all concerned. If you genuinely have a problem with certain foods or are devoted to a particular eating regime, let your host have plenty of time to sort something for you. The vegan who has failed to mention their utter devotion to vegetables before the meal is served is not going to be popular when the hosts put their best leg of lamb forward. If you have a medical problem with certain foods that is also worth mentioning. If you have so many food issues that any meal is a nightmare, you might want to consider staying at home.

It is said that King Louis XIV once had very bad toothache. His dentist decided to solve this by pulling out the offending tooth and in the process damaged the king's upper jaw and palate. Ever after, Louis struggled with soup, finding that when he drank it came out of his nose. Anyone inviting the French Sun King to supper might have done well to leave soup off the menu and he would have been polite to mention it.

Cancelling at the last minute
Don't.

Unexpectedly bringing a friend
Again, don't. Having said that, I was the friend who was brought unexpectedly to dinner and I am now married to the person who was cooking that night.

When to arrive
It's up to the host to be clear what time guests should arrive but it's up to the guests not to be so early that they risk seeing the host in his pants. Be on time or at least within fifteen minutes of the appointed hour. Being 'fashionably late' is just annoying and not at all fashionable. If you are going to be later than fifteen minutes ring and say so. Arrive clean and neat.

What to bring

Always ask your host if there is anything you can bring. I was once invited to dinner at the comedian Jeremy Hardy's house so I texted to see if he wanted me to bring anything. He texted back the single word 'Dinner'. Most hosts will reply 'Just bring yourselves'. What they actually mean is 'just bring yourself and a decent bottle of wine'. The usual gift is something that won't last but is welcome. If you don't drink bring chocolates. Flowers can be annoying as the host has to rummage about under the sink for a vase.

Think about the host. Flowers – asthma? Chocolate – diabetic? Wine – recently done for drink-driving which was in all the papers?

Being in someone's home

Where you are and are not welcome is easy – it's the old thresholds again. In general they are easy to spot as they tend to be actual thresholds.

- Don't go in the front door until invited.

- Don't go into someone's bedroom unless you know them very well indeed.

- Don't use the bathroom without asking and when you do don't open the cupboards. This is a dinner invitation not a free-for-all.

Seating plan

Don't take a seat unless indicated by the host. Family members sometimes have favourite seats at home and may feel odd even at a round table if you sit in 'their place'.

It is quite likely that you won't be seated next to your partner. This is fine, as the whole point of eating out is to meet other people not have the same conversations that you have at home. If you don't like it stay at home.

Sit down with the least amount of fuss. In Louis XIV's court (you're learning a lot about him – rules about everything, terrible soup-eater) there was a particular method for a gentleman to sit down. First he had to slide his left foot forward in front of his right, then he put both hands on the side of the chair and lowered himself gently into place. The reason was simple. If he didn't, he might split his very tight trousers. Fortunately people are able to be a little more relaxed these days but there are still a few things to think about when 'in company'.

Eating

If you are a guest at a dinner party then you are probably not a child. If you have pre-warned a host about a particular dietary problem and that has been catered for, then you should be able to eat whatever is put in front of you, however challenging. I was once served a faggot the size of a baby's head. It had never occurred to me that someone might think this melange of offcuts and offal was suitable for a dinner party so I hadn't mentioned it as being something I wouldn't want to eat. I soldiered through it and did not die.

Wait for the host or hostess to start eating. They are probably exhausted from the stress of organising the dinner and need their strength. Don't offer someone a 'taste' of your food unless you know them extremely well and are sitting next to them. Shoving a fork full of hot runny food across the table is not going to be popular.

Salt and pepper

Taste the food first. Have some faith in your host's ability to prepare a meal. If you do feel you need seasoning don't, as it were, make a meal of it.

I have a delightful friend who recently ordered a rather expensive sideboard for her home which she referred to as a *credenza* – which is of course the correct term. What she did not know is that the word comes from the Italian for 'belief'. In the sixteenth century it referred to the pre-tasting of food and drink by a servant to make sure his lord was not about to be poisoned. Eventually the word came to describe the piece of furniture which held the food before it was finally served. If pre-tasting is necessary in someone's home you may want to reconsider your friends.

Speed of eating

To consume whole pieces of food at a gulp is for storks and buffoons.

Erasmus (you remember), 1530

Tricky. Try to follow the pace of the host. Too slow and people will think you don't like the food. Too fast and you are clearly afraid you are not going to get enough. English people will immediately guess you went to boarding school.

Second helpings

Wait to be asked. Don't just take.

Clearing the plates

If it is a dinner party in someone's house then it is nice to offer but expect to be refused.

Saying thank you

Your host has hopefully made an effort and it's good to be grateful. Even if they have made no effort at all it is kind to pretend they have and that you are grateful. No Dane would ever leave even the family table without saying *Tak for mad* – thank you for the food – to which the host or parent replies *Velbekommen* – well may it become you. These days a further thanks by text is nice but a handwritten one is classy. Ideally it needs to be done the next day.

Leaving

A bit like being a comedian, timing here is everything. The trick is not to leave too late or too early. Sometimes the moment to leave is very clear. I once attended a military dinner where coffee was served after the meal in the drawing room. The general in charge and his wife drank theirs standing up, and it was clear that no one was to make themselves comfortable. We all departed shortly afterwards although no one said a word about the time.

This method would no doubt look odd in an ordinary home but there are easy cues a host can give to indicate that time is up.

'It was so nice of you to come,' 'I have so enjoyed this evening', 'We must see you again', etc., all suggest that the pleasure is now over.

The most important thing is to be subtle about the hour. Don't check your watch or your phone at the dinner table. People will think you are bored.

Don't take forever over 'goodbye'. Once you have indicated you are going to leave don't start a new anecdote. I was once at a dinner with ... see what I mean?

RESTAURANTS

Ladies travelling alone will request the escort of a waiter from the dining-room door to the table.

Ladies will make up their minds quickly as to what dishes to order.

Collier's Cyclopaedia of Commercial and Social Information and Treasury of Useful and Entertaining Knowledge on Art, Science Pastimes, Belles-lettres, and Many Other Subjects of Interest in the American Home Circle, 1882

Many years ago an actress acquaintance of mine came to London for the first time. Born and brought up in the Welsh countryside, she had an exciting job in the theatre and was both thrilled and terrified. Her new producer decided to treat her by taking her to lunch in a very smart restaurant. The night before, she phoned her mother in a panic because she had hardly ever eaten in a restaurant and was worried she wouldn't know what to order. 'Have the special,' counselled her mother, 'then you can't go wrong.' The actress arrived the next day looking as smart as she could manage and sat down in the vast restaurant. She opened the menu and saw a large box which declared 'Special Today' followed by a foreign name which she didn't recognise. When the waiter came to take the order she calmly pointed to it and said, 'I'll have that.'

'I'm afraid you can't, madam,' the waiter quietly replied. 'That's the band.'

Before we begin . . .

Eating out goes in phases. There was a time in the 1950s and 1960s when a meal in a restaurant was just for high days and holidays. Now people dine outside the home all the time, but this is not something new. In ancient Rome many houses didn't have kitchens so meals were taken at small restaurant-bars called *thermopolia*. A typical *thermopolium* had L-shaped counters. People sat here socialising and eating hot or cold food from the large storage jars sunk into the counter. There was clearly competition among the *thermopolia* owners. In Pompeii alone you can find 158 of them along the main axis of the town and near the public spaces.

Paris is often cited as the birthplace of the restaurant, but before people went out for steak frites there were thousands of informal places to get food.

Separate tables

At first people sat at communal tables and ate whatever the host decided to serve. Gradually some people who had more money wanted more choice about what they ate and whose elbow, even when not resting on the table, they rubbed when they ate it. Restaurants began before the French Revolution but they flourished when the chefs and staff of the aristocracy were looking for employment. After all the stress of so many people losing their heads the survivors also wanted to have fun and celebrate. Francis Blagdon, an English traveller writing in 1803, was amazed by his dining experience at the Parisian restaurant of a man called Beauvilliers.

> Good heaven! the bill of fare is a printed sheet of double folio, of the size of an English newspaper. It will require half an hour at least to con over this important catalogue. Let us see; Soups, thirteen sorts. –Hors-d'oeuvres, twenty-two species. –Beef, dressed in eleven different ways. –Pastry, containing fish, flesh and fowl, in eleven shapes. –Poultry and game, under thirty-two various forms. –Veal, amplified into twenty-two distinct articles. –Mutton, confined to seventeen only. –Fish, twenty-three varieties. –Roast meat, game, and

poultry, of fifteen kinds. –Entremets, or side-dishes, to the number of forty-one articles. –Desert, thirty-nine. –Wines, including those of the liqueur kind, of fifty-two denominations, besides ale and porter. –Liqueurs, twelve species, together with coffee and ices.

The word restaurant comes from the French *restaurer* meaning to 'restore or refresh'. It's a place to make you feel better. In fact during the Middle Ages and Renaissance it was common to study medicine and food preparation together. All the usual rules about table manners apply in restaurants but there are a few other matters to address as well. The first thing to remember in any eating establishment is that …

1. You belong. Do not get stressed

Don't be put off by anyone treating you as anything other than a valued customer. It might help you to feel comfortable if you make sure it's the right place for you first.

2. Make sure you can afford it

It may sound obvious but it helps if you are confident that the prices at a restaurant are within your range. Menus are often available online or the restaurant will email one to you. If you really want to go somewhere expensive but finances are stretched, then you can have dinner somewhere cheaper and just go for dessert and coffee.

On my twenty-first birthday I took some friends to London's theatrical restaurant Joe Allen's. It was May 1979 and, although it's hard to believe now, at the time the maximum amount of money you could take out of a cash machine was £25. I was a student and it was also the maximum amount of money I had. There were six of us and everyone ordered what they liked. When the bill came it amounted to exactly £25. I left all the money I had on the table and headed for the door, only to find I was being chased by the waiter.

'Where is my tip?' he shouted, 'Where is my tip?'

'I don't have any more money,' I explained mortified.

He wagged his finger at me. 'Don't you ever come in here again. I will know your face.'

His manners were appalling but it was about twenty years before I returned.

3. If you are the host make sure the restaurant is right for everyone invited

A steak place is unlikely to work well for a vegan. Check the dietary requirements of your group before you make a booking. If there are a lot of you (more than eight) think about the kind of restaurant in which that will work. Big groups usually make a big noise. Some restaurants won't take such large bookings unless you use a private dining room. Don't be offended if they say no. The same is true about small children. Expensive restaurants may not have high chairs and certainly won't want anyone colouring in or playing with toy cars at the table. You may be sitting next to a couple who have saved for a very important romantic meal. Don't spoil it for them with a vision of the horror of eating with kids which is to come. One of your Top Cs – *Consideration*.

4. Getting a table

Make sure you book well ahead (about two weeks for the best places although there are restaurants like *Noma* in Copenhagen which only take bookings once a month). Let the restaurant know in advance if you have particular needs, such as a table suitable for a wheelchair user. If you haven't booked and the place looks empty do not doubt the maître d' when he says it is full – most places have timed reservations and the place may fill up any minute.

5. Dealing with waiters

If someone offers to take your coat, let them. Do not leave it on the back of your chair for the staff to trip over. If you are ready to order, shut your menu and put it down. The waiter can then see from a distance that you are not still trying to decide. People who are imperious with waiters always suggest that they were once waiters themselves and wish to prove how far they have risen. Never shout. Your words with waiters should be requests not commands. The staff are on their feet all day or night serving food. You are sitting down and enjoying yourself. Have some empathy.

If you have to send food back remember that the waiter didn't prepare it. He or she will not be best pleased with the kitchen either. A good restaurant will want to know what is wrong and try to make amends. Allow them the opportunity to do so rather than dashing off a critical online review on your phone.

6. Ordering

If you are not sure about something on the menu ask the waiter. It's his/her job to help you. The first restaurants in Paris only served soup. Now life is a little more complicated and you can't be expected to know every ingredient or dish possible. It's fine to ask. Better to ask than order something you don't want. But do order something. Anything – do not say you are not hungry and then eat everyone else's food. If you are really not hungry it is fine to order two starters. It is not fine to have two main courses. If you have serious food allergies ring ahead and warn the chef. I have ordered very complex dishes for friends who are intolerant to almost every ingredient imaginable and had very nice food served.

I had a friend who refused to ask for help in any eating establishment. This included restaurants in countries where she didn't really speak the language. She was once in a Spanish cantina and insisted on ordering for herself and three guests in Spanish despite not being fluent in the language. She gave her order and the waiter said in perfect English, 'Are you sure?' My friend was outraged at his impertinence and dismissed him with a wave of her hand. A short while later the waiter returned bearing a silver platter with two dozen fried eggs. So determined not to be wrong my pal waited till he had put them down and gone back to the kitchen before silently putting all twenty-four eggs in her handbag.

7. Focus on the meal

It's just like eating anywhere. You know the routine. Turn off your mobile phone. Don't brush your hair, pick your teeth, apply make-up or text people who are not with you. Don't be excused so many times that people become concerned about your health or check to see if you have a drug habit. Go between courses not during. Don't tell people you're going to the toilet. Just say 'excuse me' as you get up.

8. Don't rush

If you have taken the time to choose a nice place to eat then don't be in a hurry. Let your fellow diners take their time in choosing what they want to eat. It's supposed to be a treat, not a fuel stop.

9. If someone comes over to talk to you – stand up

Don't stay seated. You are not a medieval king.

10. The end of the meal

Plates should not be cleared till everyone at the table has finished. It is fine to ask staff to wait if they begin to clear plates early. If you have signalled for the bill without success then getting up to leave will quietly get you the attention you desire.

The wretched bill – whose shout is it?

* If you invited everyone then you should pay.

* If everyone is sharing the bill make the arrangements before you go in. Don't go for a group meal if you are not prepared to split the cost. It is, however, kind to choose somewhere that everyone can afford.

* Don't be the person who argues over every penny at a group meal. It's very boring and you are unlikely to be invited again.

* Don't assume that just because your friend is a higher earner than you that they will pay the bill.

* Going Dutch is fine with friends but you might think it nicer to take turns treating each other.

- If you are determined to treat someone and don't want a fight over the bill you can leave your credit card with the maître d' when you arrive.

Basic tips

Nothing, if you are dissatisfied with something, but make sure you are clear what it was so you don't just look mean. Remember the waiter is probably someone trying to get a break in an entirely different career. He/she is probably not very well paid.

10 per cent = ordinary service
15 per cent = good service
20 per cent = heavenly everything

Doggy bag

When they were filled, he said unto his disciples,
Gather up the fragments that remain, that nothing be lost.

John 6:12. Jesus on the subject of leftovers after the loaves and fishes meal

The doggy bag or container of leftover food taken by a customer from a restaurant meal is more common in the United States than in the UK. I was once served an absurdly large steak in a very smart restaurant in New York City. Although I was staying in a hotel and didn't want the leftover meat I knew there were a number of homeless people who waited outside to be give doggy bags. I duly had my excess meat bagged up to give away. Out in the street it was cold and I approached a man with my offering, feeling rather virtuous. 'Would you like this?' I proffered my full bag of food. 'What is it?' he enquired. 'Steak' I answered, slightly surprised. 'T-bone' I added, as if that made it better. He shook his head. 'No thanks,' he said. 'I'm Catholic, it's Friday. I'll wait for fish.'

It was a lesson to me to remember that everyone, no matter their circumstance, can have standards.

Doggy bags are not something new. When a Roman guest

brought with him his own piece of material or *mappa* to use as a napkin, he expected it on departure to be filled with delicacies leftover from the feast. Some British restaurants can still be a little sniffy about the practice but there is no harm in asking.

ATTENDING A BANQUET

Never trust a man in a ready-made bow tie.

Claus Toksvig (1929–88), Danish broadcaster, my father

Formal dinners are usually held as a kind of ritual or theatre. They often celebrate transitions in life such as births, christenings and marriages, mark particular occasions or recognise the work of a particular industry. Eating together is a commemorative moment. I have a Jewish friend who describes the many festivals she and her family mark as being summed up historically as 'They tried to kill us, we survived, let's eat'.

An aperitif

At this sort of meal it is common to be offered a drink before the meal. The word 'aperitif' comes from the Latin *aperitivus*, meaning 'opener'. Drinks served before dinner often consist of spirits and are usually stronger than those served with the meal. They are intended to stimulate conversation and to help the body prepare for food. They are not there for you to get bladdered. Anyone who gets drunk before dinner is not going to appreciate the meal. It's also not great to over-consume at the table. In my native Denmark when I was a child everyone drank at the same pace. People only touched their alcoholic beverage during a toast. There was, as I recall, always an endless series of toasts.

The place setting

If napkins are distributed, yours should be placed on the left shoulder or arm; goblet and knife go to the right, bread to the left.

Erasmus, *De civilitate morum puerilium*, 1530

Fewer people give formal dinners these days so the chances are you'll be a guest rather than a host. The first time you attend a formal meal you may feel a little overwhelmed by the range of cutlery and glassware in front of you. You may worry that you might eat someone else's bread by mistake or take a gulp of their wine. First of all, never gulp wine; but to help you recall which bits on the table belong to you, all you need to know is that –

Solids on the left: liquids are on the right

I was taught an easy way to remember – make the symbol for OK with both hands. The left hand makes a 'b' for bread while the right makes a 'd' for drinks. If you are going to do this at the table do it in your lap. In parts of Europe the gesture can be offensive and in several South American countries it suggests the person you are gesturing to is a homosexual. The person may well be a homosexual but may not want it pointed out at the dinner table.

Bread

It's quite common at a formal meal for a roll to already be on your bread plate when you sit down (that'll be the one on your left). If a basket is passed it is passed to the right by the host. (The host should offer it to the person on their immediate left first so they don't have to wait for it to go all the way round the table first but really, let's not get hung up on all this. It's just bread.)

The rules for rolls:

- **Only take one roll at a time.**
- **Use the butter knife.** Slice butter from the butter dish with the small knife provided and put it on your own bread plate. This stops the butter dish filling up with breadcrumbs as it is

passed around. Put the butter knife back on the butter dish before passing it on. If the butter is in foil (urgh), unwrap it, fold the empty foil so you can't get it stuck to your sleeve and put it at the side of the plate.

- **Cut rolls with a knife at breakfast, break them with your hands at dinner.** I'm not sure why, but at an evening meal break them open with your hands before buttering. Hold a small piece with your fingers and butter it with your butter knife. Do this one piece at a time.

- **Do not use bread as a mop.** Do not use your bread to wipe gravy or anything else from your plate. You can't be that famished. You will spill.

Seating plan

Where there are no women there are no good manners.

Johann Wolfgang von Goethe (1749–1832), German writer

At a formal dinner there should either be a list displayed showing where you are sitting or someone will indicate this to you. It is still the norm at formal events for men and women to be seated in alternate seats. As someone in a civil partnership I have caused many a headache for the organisers of such an event who find they need to invite a male couple as well in order to make the numbers work. This gender balanced seating arrangement probably dates back to the Crusades which took place between AD 1000 and 1300. In order to teach knights manners they were often paired with a lady at dinner. The females had a civilising effect as the men learnt not to lick their fingers, smack their lips or snort. Any woman sitting next to a man at a formal meal knows she is there to keep him in check.

Place cards are used when there are more than eight people who don't know each other. It is very bad manners to switch place cards around but I have done it many times to avoid someone I really didn't relish sitting beside.

Napkins

These are laid in the centre of the plate, unless the first course is a cold dish and has already been put on the table. In that case the napkin will be to the left of the place setting. Put the napkin on your lap as soon as you sit down. If a member of staff helps you to your seat do not be surprised if they unfold the napkin for you. They will do this for everyone. You are not being singled out as being most likely to spill.

Plates

There was a time when people used to eat off a piece of stale bread called a *trencher*. At the end of the meal this could either be eaten or given to the poor. These days we prefer plates. It is possible that when you sit down there will be an empty plate at your setting which no one will ever put food on. This is called a *charger*. It will be larger than a usual dinner plate and often quite decorative. It will either be removed or the first course plate will be placed on top. They are always removed before dessert.

Food service

Where a waiter holds a tray of food for you to help yourself then food will be served from the left and plates removed from the right. That is because most people are right-handed and it is easier. Side dishes are laid to the left of the diner for the same reason. If the food has been put on the plate in the kitchen then it will be served from the right and taken from the right. These rules exist so that everyone knows what is happening and they don't accidentally get a plate of beef on the head. Gravy may be passed. If the container has a handle – when you pass it turn the handle to face the person receiving it.

If something gets spilled or broken, politely ask the staff if they can help. Don't worry. Accidents happen even to posh people.

Staff

Being nice to staff is easy and essential. They are probably being paid very little. Always say 'thank you' when they serve you

Using the right fork

The actor Errol Flynn was a man who lived life to the full. One day, while he was on his yacht, he realised that his dog had disappeared. Sadly it was discovered that the animal had drowned. Flynn was very famous and a journalist wrote a story saying that Errol had been at fault in the dog's death. Weeks later the journalist happened to be in the same nightclub as Flynn, who decided to beat the man up. The reporter's wife saw them fighting and stabbed Flynn in the ear with a piece of cutlery. The whole thing went to court but eventually they all became friends with Flynn declaring to the journalist, 'Your wife has good table manners; she used the right fork.'

something. Lothar Herzog was butler to Erich Honecker, the leader of socialist East Germany, for twelve years. He said that Honecker ate with his mouth open, slurping and burping as he drank West German beer. Honecker never once had a conversation with his servant. It's worth remembering that the former leader ended his life in exile.

Cutlery

Even if there seem to be a lot of different implements it is not complicated. Start with the cutlery furthest away from your plate and work your way in towards the middle. If you are still in doubt watch your host, whose job it is to silently indicate what you need to do. Don't worry too much about it. Anyone who makes a big deal out of you using the wrong implement is very bad-mannered.

Some snobs used to believe that having many rows of cutlery showed off their status. This is no longer necessary and I trust we've established that fish knives are absurd.

Finger bowl

One of the first jokes I remember learning as a child was told in Danish. It related the story of an elderly couple from the country attending their first formal meal. They had just finished eating some unshelled prawns when the waiter put down a small bowl of water beside them with a piece of lemon floating in it. 'What the hell is that?' muttered the old man. 'Shut up,' replied his wife, 'and drink your lemon soup.'

Finger bowls are an ancient idea. The Bayeux Tapestry (which is actually an embroidery and not a tapestry at all) depicts a *ewerer*, a servant with a variety of tasks, kneeling before the high table with a finger bowl and napkin. They are not as popular as they used to be (the bowls, not the ewerers, although you don't get so many ewerers either) but they may well be offered if the meal has been a challenging one for cleanliness. If someone puts a warm bowl of water next to you, rinse the tips of your fingers and wipe them on your napkin.

Finger bowls are an exception to the rule about liquids. They are placed on the left in order that you cannot confuse it with liquids which are for drinking. If it's on your left it is not lemon soup.

Drinking

My rule of life prescribed as an absolutely sacred rite smoking cigars and also the drinking of alcohol before, after and if need be during all meals and in the intervals between them.

Winston Churchill (1874–1965), British prime minister

Glasses

The water glass is usually the one directly above your knife. The wine glasses will be to the right of the water glass. The clue as to which is which is the size.

* Larger wine glass – red
* Smaller wine glass – white
* Champagne is served in a tall, flute glass

If you are not sure, wait until someone else pours. If you are wearing lipstick blot your lips on your napkin before you drink to avoid staining the glass. If you are dying of thirst and can't wait for someone to pour, you may want to get a check-up.

Wine

Champagne is the only wine that leaves a woman beautiful after drinking it.

Madame de Pompadour (1721–64),
official chief mistress to Louis XV

There used to be a notion that wine should be served 'white before red, light before heavy, young before old' and white wine is usually offered with the starter or appetiser. These days most people are a little more relaxed. White wine will be served in the smaller of the two wine glasses and should be held by the stem of the glass. Because white wine is traditionally served chilled this stops it becoming warmed by your hand.

Red wine is often served with the main course and it requires a larger glass because it needs 'to breathe'. It too should be held by the stem. This allows you to enjoy the colour of the wine and stops your finger marks getting on the glass.

Don't pour your own drink even if the bottle is in front of you.

If the wine is being served by staff it will be served from the right. If you don't want any, it is perfectly acceptable to turn your wine glass upside down to indicate you would rather be passed over. This is much better than making a big deal out of it. Don't clap your hand on top of the glass. The waiter may miss the cue and pour wine on you.

A good guest ought to know how much drink they can consume. Being drunk is never attractive. On the whole society contains the use of alcohol by seeing it as something consumed at specific times. People have a drink after work but rarely during. All cultures have rules about alcohol although alcohol addiction and bad behaviour spurred on by drinking seems to be a very Western phenomenon. The Camba people of Bolivia drink a rum that is 180 per cent proof and yet in their society it causes 'no arguments, no disputes, no sexual aggression, no verbal aggression' and most of all, no alcoholism. Would that the same could be said for drinking at European dinner parties.

It is perfectly acceptable and, indeed, commendable to declare that you don't want a drink because you are driving.

Being excused

Most formal meals will have what is called a 'comfort break'. This is usually announced and is the time when people excuse themselves to powder their nose or just get away from a challenging dinner companion. Ideally you shouldn't excuse yourself during a meal unless it is a comfort break. Again common sense comes into play. It's not worth becoming ill. For many years the death of Tycho Brahe, the Danish astronomer in 1601, was held up as an example of what can happen to you if you worry about etiquette at a banquet. He was said to have remained at table whilst desperate for a pee and later died at a banquet from a strained bladder. He did stay seated when he shouldn't have but more recently there has been a suggestion that in fact he died from mercury poisoning due to the metals used to create his prosthetic nose.

This brings up a rare additional rule for formal meals – if you are sitting with someone who has a fake, metallic nose – don't mention it.

Showing that you have finished

It is very rude to clear someone's plate who hasn't finished. To give you an idea how seriously the ancient Romans took this rule – they believed the clearing of someone's plate who hadn't completed his meal would mean the diner's sudden death. Queen Victoria clearly didn't know this. She ate very quickly and plates were cleared as soon as she was finished. This often meant some people hadn't even been served yet and didn't get to eat at all. It also shows that being born with a silver spoon in your mouth doesn't necessarily mean you know how to behave.

Coffee

Coffee cups are usually laid out after the meal. If the cup is already on the table it will be on the right. If you have stirred your coffee, always take your spoon out of the cup. If you don't you could have your eye out and cause a mess on the carpet. Place the spoon in the saucer. If there is no saucer then it is not a formal meal and you have been misled.

Cheese

As a matter of course, young ladies do not eat cheese at dinner-parties.

> *Manners and Rules of Good Society* by 'A Member of the Aristocracy', 1888

The anonymous aristocrat doesn't give a reason why. Maybe it gave young ladies bad breath. There is some fun to be had thinking of the horror one might have caused by spearing a piece of gorgonzola with the wrong knife and handing it to a woman.

Women can now help themselves but no one should take the 'nose of the cheese'. As the French say, 'jamais le nez' but what is that? It's the pointed end of a triangle of cheese. Posh cheeses are usually made in a round shape and the centre will be the richest part. The nose of the cheese is thought to be the most delicious and it would be rude to take all of the best bit. Slice a triangle of cheese like a cake by taking a sliver from the side.

The cheese knife is yet another Victorian invention. Some of them were excellent, such as the flushing toilet and the telephone. The cheese knife, however, was unnecessary.

If someone asks you to pass them a small piece of cheese, spear it with your knife and pass it.

Fruit

Fruit should be eaten ripe, raw, fresh and perfect. It should be eaten in moderation. It should be eaten not later than four o'clock in the afternoon.

The Road to Happy Old Age, Dr William Whitty Hall (1869)

Fruit can be tricky to eat politely. The headmistress at my English boarding school had very strict ideas about eating almost anything. She once told me that a gentlewoman at the dinner table should 'never embark upon an orange'.

At a formal meal all fruit should be eaten where possible with a knife and fork. So, if you must have a banana, peel it and then eat it with your cutlery. Melon is unlikely to be served unless it has already been prepared in the kitchen ready for you to eat easily with a knife and fork. If it hasn't, then the meal is less impressive than you had hoped.

- **Large and medium-sized fruit** – needs to be quartered with your knife and then eaten with your fork.

- **Small fresh fruit** – such as plums – can be eaten with your fingers but they are best avoided as you're probably wearing quite smart clothing. If you insist on a plum or anything else with a stone, eat as much of the fruit as possible then cup your hand over your mouth, push the stone forward with your tongue and put it discreetly on your plate.

- **Fruit with pits** – such as cherries – would be unusual at a formal occasion. Put them in your mouth with a spoon, eat round the pit and then put it back on the spoon and down onto the plate. Don't be tempted to show people that you can tie a knot in a cherry stem with your tongue no matter how much this impresses your family.

- **Small fruits with pips** – such as grapes. Discreetly remove the seeds from your mouth into your cupped hand and put them on your plate.

- **Embarking upon an orange** (if you really must)
  The orange is an hesperidium which is a berry with a thick
  rind. Try to distract attention from your attempts to eat it by
  telling your dinner companion this.

  - Cut off each end of the rind.
  - Cut the peel off in strips.
  - Remove any pips with the tip of your knife.
  - Divide the orange into segments. These are actually
    called carpels and again you may need this information
    for conversation while you struggle.
  - Eat.
  - Use your napkin on your chin.
  - Check your chin surreptitiously with your fingers.
  - Do not ask your companion to do this.

Buffet

Never overload your plate as it makes you look greedy. It's worth
remembering Adolf Frederick, King of Sweden, who has the
distinction of being known as 'the king who ate himself to death'.
He died on 12 February 1771 having managed a meal of lobster,
caviar, sauerkraut, smoked herring and champagne, followed by
fourteen servings of his favourite dessert, *hetvägg*, which is a bun
served in a bowl of hot milk.

It is better to take less and then think about returning for
seconds.

Behaving badly or playing the fool at dinner

You can't be truly rude until you understand good manners.

Rita Mae Brown, American author

It's worth bearing in mind that entertaining at dinner used to be a
professional job. Henry II of England gave an estate (and by that
I mean land and not a car big enough for kids and a dog) to his
jester, Roland le Pettour, because he was so amusing. In return

he was expected to turn up at the king's annual Christmas Day banquet to perform *saltum, siffletum et pettum* or *bumbulum* which translates as 'a leap, a whistle and a fart'. Today you would need to have some courage to get away with this if people are still going to like you afterwards. Make sure you have enough lovable personality to carry it off.

This is not to say that playing the fool must never be done. It is true that life is for living and rules are sometimes there to be broken, as Elizaveta Petrovna made clear. Elizaveta lived in the eighteenth century and was one of only two surviving children of Catherine I of Russia. Catherine was quite a girl. She began life as a housemaid and never learnt to read. Nevertheless she went on to become empress and was the first woman to rule Imperial Russia. She had clear ideas about alcohol and declared that no gentleman should be inebriated before 9 p.m. and no lady should ever be in such a state. Princess Elizaveta disliked this rule. Ignoring the fact that critics were accusing her of being responsible for the 'corruption of morals' (the sort of behaviour every parent dreads), Elizaveta and her pals managed a good time by dressing as men and holding transvestite balls.

You need panache for bad behaviour. The nineteenth-century novelist, Lady Caroline Lamb, once had herself served entirely naked in a soup tureen as a birthday gift for Queen Victoria's prime minister, Lord Melbourne. This is not an easy gift to carry off with poise. Be sure you are confident that stepping outside the usual restraints of behaviour isn't just going to leave you (and everyone else) mortified. Nevertheless, if you can do it, good luck to you.

Heavens, that was an awful lot to digest. It mostly boils down to keeping clean, staying sober and making sure everyone is happy. There is, however, one critical bit we need to add. Only the strictest monks eat and drink in silence. Now we are gathered we need to begin to think about what on earth we're going to say to each other.

Much love

Sandi

4: COMMUNICATION

Be not deceived: evil communications corrupt good manners.

Apostle Paul, 1 Corinthians

Dear Mary

Before we widen our circle even further, let's take a quick look at how we communicate with others. I have to be honest, I'm not entirely sure about that quote from St Paul. I agree with the basic principle that how we communicate with people matters, but I struggle a little with the saint himself. Apart from being endlessly judgemental he also wrote interminable letters to the Corinthians and as far as we know not one of them ever bothered to write back. Anyway, the basic premise is right – how you communicate says something about what kind of person you are.

There was a time when good communication involved the correct employment of consonants when speaking and a good quality pen with some nice stationery when writing. Today things are a little more complicated, so let's start with basics before we take a deep breath and look at what modern technology has done to the world.

CONVERSATION

Speak clearly, if you speak at all;
carve every word before you let it fall.

Oliver Wendel Holmes (1809–94), American author

Oh dear, more Latin incoming but I'll be quick. The word 'conversation' comes from the Latin *conversationem* and it means the 'act of living with'. The critical part of conversation is that it is not a monologue. Ideally it is two or more people verbalising and sharing their thoughts. You need to listen as much as you need to speak. This means ...

1. Consider with whom you are having a conversation

Decide, in fact, if they are the sort of person who would like you using a word such as 'whom'. If you are meeting someone for the first time, try to find some mutual area of interest. This may seem obvious, but my experience suggests it's best to avoid religion, politics, money, sex and how successful your own children are. You have no idea which buttons you might accidentally press and cause an upset. If you are a keen sports fan do not presume that everyone else is. Your friend's aged grandmother who you are meeting for the first time may be less interested in the time you lost your Capri pants at a full moon party than your friend would be. She may, of course, be a game old girl with similar experiences, but test the waters first before launching in. Fish around a little and see what they bite at.

2. Think before you speak

Oh dear, another old chestnut, but a chestnut for a reason. Try to remember if there is some information you have about the person that might suggest conversational 'no-go' areas. If someone has suffered a bereavement they may not be in the mood for hilarity. Thinking before speaking also helps avoid lazy tics in your speech such as a common contemporary habit of overusing the word 'like', as in 'I was like hungry and the shop was like shut and I was like cross because they like sell cakes which I like like.'

Also be careful about jokes. They are hard to carry off and can bring a reasonable conversation to a grinding halt. It's also worth remembering that one person's hilarity may be another's political or religious trigger point. If you are in a group, be careful not to make an amusing remark about one of the other guests to someone you have just met. The chances are astonishingly high that you will be talking about their partner.

3. Consider the ox in the room

Life is not a play and you may be surprised by what someone wants to impart. Even more surprising, this may include members of your family. When the thirteenth-century philosopher Thomas Aquinas first began his studies his fellow students nicknamed him 'the dumb ox' because he was large and rather silent. One day his tutor, Albertus Magnus, spoke to him in a private session and was heard to declare, 'They call brother Thomas a dumb ox; let me tell you that one day the whole world will listen to his bellowings.' Thomas went on fundamentally to shape medieval thought and his ideas continue to influence modern philosophy. Check out what everyone has to say in case there is a dumb ox you are overlooking.

4. Help the conversation along

Don't shut down avenues of chat with negative responses. If the person you are talking to says 'Have you read any good books lately?' the answer should be anything other than 'No.' Years ago I was a regular on an improvised television show called *Whose Line is it Anyway?* The rule in improvising is that you have to 'accept and build'. If someone enters the stage and starts a scene by saying, 'Ah there you are, doctor,' the scene is not going to last long if you reply 'I'm not a doctor.'

Having a conversation is a form of improvising. Listen to what someone has said and try to build the conversation. If someone is struggling enough with you to say 'Have you read any good books lately?', the least you can do is reply, 'I'm afraid I haven't. Do you have something you could suggest?'

5. Wait your turn

Conversation is like a game of *Twister* without all the annoying physicality. You need to wait to make your move. Not everyone is the most thrilling speaker; nevertheless everyone is entitled to try to make their point. If you let someone ramble on a bit then hopefully they will extend you the same courtesy. If you are short of time, say so, but nicely – indicate you would love to hear more some other time but leave that time vague.

6. Don't correct the other person

No one likes a pedant. If they say 'less' instead of 'fewer' let it go. It's what they are saying that matters, not how they say it. Never correct anyone in public even if they deserve it. It will only draw attention to whatever gaffe they are making. If they have something in their teeth that can be mentioned quietly. So too can an open fly. When I was growing up in the States this was done by saying 'Your wing level is low and your co-pilot's hanging out'. This is not a good idea.

7. Don't lie

Nothing is more criminal, mean or ridiculous, than lying.

Chesterfield's *Principles of Politeness*

You will get caught out. It's almost guaranteed and it's not worth it. The truth is, on the whole, more interesting and much easier to remember.

8. Don't try to outdo your conversation companion

If someone is telling you about an exciting adventure they have had, don't try to top it with a better one of your own. If they have been ill and must tell you the details, you don't then need to outdo them with your own life-threatening experience.

9. Don't reveal too much about yourself

This is a conversation not a therapy session. No one on greeting requires an analysis of your current emotional state. I met someone in the street who I hadn't seen for years. 'How are you?' I enquired politely, wishing she hadn't seen me. 'I've been through a very rocky time,' she answered, 'but I think I am coming out the other side because my stars are coming into alignment.' Hard to know what to say to that, apart from 'Excellent'.

10. Talk to the person you're talking to

It all sounds so simple when you write it down. Don't look over someone's shoulder to see if there is anyone more interesting to talk to. There probably is but don't do it anyway. You would hate it if someone did that to you. Look the person you are chatting to in the eye. Give them your attention. Who knows, someday, you might need theirs. Also don't turn away or look at your watch while someone is speaking unless you are on the phone to them and they can't see. Again, focus, people, focus.

Swearing

There's no absolute rule about swearing. Even computers, once they have learnt naughty words, find it hard not to use them. All the slang words in the *Urban Dictionary* were uploaded onto the American supercomputer Watson, but had to be deleted again when it kept answering researcher's questions with the word 'bullshit'.

There have always been some words which are deemed to be more shocking than others. Interestingly, they tend to be ones with a hard, explosive sound in them, as if that has more impact. Our attitude to swearing, like so many things, changes with the times. It's not uncommon now to hear swear words being used in a sentence like a sort of verbal tic, but for those who disapprove it is worth noting that the use of foul language was at one time entirely normal for the upper classes. There is a story about Sarah Churchill, the Duchess of Marlborough in the early eighteenth century, calling unexpectedly upon her lawyer, Lord Mansfield. Mansfield was not home and she declined to leave her name. When describing the visit to his master, his Lordship's secretary is said to have declared, 'I could not make out, sir, who she was; but she swore so dreadfully that she must be a lady of quality.'

Today the rules for swearing when not at the dinner table are roughly the same as the ones when you are out and about. Be aware that some people don't like it. A lot of people swear on Twitter and that is generally accepted. However even here it is worth considering the impact. Would you walk into a train station with a megaphone and swear at a group of strangers? Well, you might if the train was on fire but perhaps not on a normal Tuesday morning heading for work. Who is going to receive your swearing?

The main thing is to be inventive about your choice of words then no one can be offended. I was once accused by the *Daily Mail* (and I confess to some pride in this) of being the 'rudest woman in Britain'. I was hosting a satirical programme about the news, *The News Quiz*, on Radio 4 where the discussion centred around the Conservative party wishing to reduce child benefit. I declared 'This is the Tories putting the N into Cuts.' It was a brilliant joke written for me by a man called Simon Littlefield. One man was outraged and persuaded the *Daily Mail* temporarily to feel the same. The problem was that everywhere I repeated the joke to assess how offensive it was it received raucous laughter. The C word (I am ashamed to tell you I have a small boat registered as *The Sea Word*) still has the power to shock, but there are times when one has to allow that it is funny.

In 1943, at the height of the Second World War, the British Ambassador to Moscow, Sir Archibald Clark Kerr, wrote the following letter to Foreign Office minister Lord Reginald Pembroke.

My Dear Reggie,

In these dark days man tends to look for little shafts of light that spill from Heaven. My days are probably darker than yours, and I need, my God I do, all the light I can get. But I am a decent fellow, and I do not want to be mean and selfish about what little brightness is shed upon me from time to time. So I propose to share with you a tiny flash that has illuminated my sombre life and tell you that God has given me a new Turkish colleague whose card tells me that he is called Mustapha Kunt.

We all feel like that, Reggie, now and then, especially when Spring is upon us, but few of us would care to put it on our cards. It takes a Turk to do that.

Sir Archibald Clerk Kerr,
H.M. Ambassador.

Conversation at the dinner table

It isn't so much what's on the table that matters, as what's on the chairs.

W. S. Gilbert (1836–1911), English author

Check out the general notes on conversation, but there are a few pointers to add which count even at the family meal. Eating at a table together is a kind of theatre and we each need to play our part. Ideally it's a visual feast as well as an actual one, where the food is presented waist high and deserves our attention and respect. It is not, however, a trough, for we are also there to spend time together. There are two kinds of diner who can be annoying:

1. The one who is too loud and dominates the conversation.

2. The one who says nothing and sits like a sort of 'Bermuda Triangle' sucking the life out of the occasion.

Try not to be either. There are some easy rules about chow chatter:

1. Do not have the television on

The word 'focus' comes from the Latin *focus* meaning 'hearth' or 'fireplace'. It's a word which originally stood for home and family. We are still comforted by an open fire in a pub or an old house because it feels 'so homely'. Eating together creates community, and focusing on the people you are sharing with is both a pleasure and a necessity. Even for an ordinary work-day family meal it is nice just to catch up and it's an essential way for parents to know what is happening in their children's lives. Sitting together and asking everyone how their day has been is a critical part of checking up on each other. Get to know your kids; you might even like them.

2. Don't whisper

If you have something private to say to someone, do it away from the dinner table. It's that old communal thing again – we're all supposed to be eating and chatting together.

3. Do mind your language

(Check the general notes on swearing.) Some people don't like it and they can't get away from it as you sit confined to the table. Mostly it's incredibly lazy. It shows a disregard for the incredible complexity of the English language. There are more than a million words at your disposal with which you might express irritation or fury. If you must swear do at least be inventive. *'Thou art an artless, crook-pated, fawning, mewling, elf-skinned puttock'* is so much more interesting than those four-letter words that everyone knows. It might even start a conversation.

4. Don't make inappropriate conversation whilst eating

If poking at the leg of a rabbit stew don't say it reminds you of your pet cat as a child. The reason meat comes nicely packaged at the supermarket is that most people don't want to think about the animal it came from.

5. Avoid arguments

It is odd to think that one might have to 'bite one's tongue' during a meal but there is nothing more calculated to give you an upset stomach than fighting while eating. If one of your in-laws has rather extreme political views it is a thought to avoid mentioning the subject over dinner. It is also worth considering how many meals in the future you may have to share with them.

If you do get heated about something, never gesture with your cutlery. You may make your point felt in an unintended manner.

6. Make sure everyone gets a turn to speak

There is always one person who tries to dominate the conversation in a group. Help the younger or less confident diner to join in by asking them, for example, 'and what do you think about that?'.

If they're really shy maybe ask something that doesn't require too great an answer.

7. Join in

The people you live with are your 'home team'. Keep them on side.

Conversation at a formal meal

Here you need to follow all the usual rules about chatting at table whilst ensuring that you spend time speaking with the dinner companions either side of you. If you know who you are going to sit next to before the meal then it may be worth spending a little time finding out something about them. This needs to be general information and not something that suggests the stalker in you. So …

1. Be prepared

If you are shy, try to think of a few things to say before you sit down. *The Deipnosophists*, or 'Sophists at Dinner', is a lengthy and fictitious account written by Athenaeus of Naucratis in the early third century AD about a dinner held with twenty-two learned men. During the meal the men cover every kind of topic in their chat, ranging from literature to botany and the arts. You don't need to be that clever. When I was a child we used to be told to read the first three pages of *The Times* plus the obituaries before sitting down to dinner. I doubt it is advice handed to anyone now, but it is not a bad idea to know what is happening in the world. The internet is a fantastically fast way to get the headlines.

2. Use the 'interview' technique

The art of conversation consists as much in listening politely as in talking agreeably.

Eliza Cheadle, *Manners of Modern Society* (1872)

There is no topic anyone finds more fascinating than themselves. Ask your new companion about themselves, their work, their home and so on as you search for some common ground for conversation that you both find interesting.

This method would have been helpful to the young American woman who, in 1921, sat next to Chinese ambassador Wellington Koo. Koo was representing his country at the Washington Naval Conference in the US capital. At a banquet he was seated beside a young woman who could initially think of nothing to say. The meal was served and this finally stimulated her to enquire of her distinguished companion, 'Likee soupee?' Koo nodded and carried on eating. At the end of the meal he was asked to address the guests which he did at length and in perfect English. As he sat down he turned to the hapless girl and asked 'Likee speechee?'

A formal meal probably gives you a chance to chat to someone which will never come again. I once sat next to the Crown Princess of Spain at a dinner. I can't say we had much in common but I knew it was a one-off in my life and enjoyed finding out as much about her as possible. To be honest it wasn't much. Nevertheless, don't miss a once in a lifetime opportunity. There is a tale told about the father of Peter Pan, J. M. Barrie, being seated next to the poet A. E. Housman at a dinner. Barrie loved Housman's work and had longed to meet him, yet he hardly spoke. When he got home he wrote to Housman saying, 'Dear Professor Houseman, I am sorry about last night, when I sat next to you and did not say a word. You must have thought I was a very rude man: I am really a very shy man. Sincerely yours, J. M. Barrie.'

I'm not sure Housman behaved very well, for he immediately replied: 'Dear Sir James Barrie, I am sorry about last night, when I sat next to you and did not say a word. You must have thought I was a very rude man: I am really a very shy man. Sincerely yours, A. E. Housman. P.S. And now you've made it worse for you have spelt my name wrong.'

3. Avoiding unpleasant topics

You don't have to talk about something you find disagreeable or boring. Change the subject, decline to pursue the matter by saying it's not your specialist area or you don't remember anything about it. If the person decides to reveal something difficult that has happened to them, the best thing to say is 'I'm sorry'.

4. Don't be a bore

Hard as it may be to believe, it is possible that other people may not match your enthusiasm for your own children and their 'hilarious' or 'cute' exploits, nor may they be all that intrigued by details about your latest illness. Not everyone is interested in your pet subject. I was once out to dinner with a sports journalist (sadly, good manners prevent me from naming her) whose utter obsession with horses couldn't even have been excused if she had been bred from one which, I have to be honest, I began to suspect. As we sat with our menus she banged on and on about some 'filly' she thought was rather fine. As someone who applauds the invention of the car, her equine passion mystified me, but I sat in respectful silence. At last the waiter came to take our order. 'Excellent,' I declared, 'Let's put the *à la carte* before the horse.' I looked up to a blank stare and had a certain sense of tumbleweed whirling across the restaurant. She went back to the horse and I realised I was in for a long evening.

Persuading a bore to change tack is tricky. Perhaps the best route is to put your hands up and say 'I am overwhelmed by your knowledge on this subject. It's brilliant. Do you know anything about ...?' And then pick an alternative topic.

Nothing too personal or demanding, please.

WRITING

Writing was invented a few thousand years ago when business became too complicated for one person to remember. One can only imagine that the first missives were less than enthralling. The basic rule to recall is that you should reply in the same manner in which you were addressed. Thus if someone emails you to say there has been a death in the family it's on the whole best not to reply by letter. Letters are, however, lovely and too often overlooked.

Letters

There are whole books published to give you very precise rules about how to address bishops, royalty and other folk you are unlikely to correspond with on a regular basis, so I'll just deal with a few basics.

1. Sometimes a letter is the only form of communication

If someone you know has suffered a bereavement or loss, one of the kindest things you can do is to handwrite a letter. Your hand-writing is entirely personal to you. It is your own unique work of art and it shows you took the time to think of some words of comfort or condolence. Handwritten letters are also wonderful mementos of great occasions, so a letter sent from a parent to a child on the occasion of their graduation or wedding or some other benchmark in life is a lovely way to express pride in them. A handwritten thank-you note indicates how much a gift has really meant to you.

2. Use nice stationery

If you are going to go to all that trouble why not choose some paper which feels nice? People are more likely to keep a hand-written letter than an email. When I was at British boarding school we had very tough, hard toilet paper which I used to substitute for airmail paper to send home to my parents in New York. I see now that it was a comment on my incarceration.

3. Date the letter

As the recipient is likely to keep your missive, make sure they can look back to see when it was sent. Remember to include the year.

4. Try to be interesting

According to Chesterfield's *Principles of Politeness* 'For gay and amusing letters there are none that equal Comte Bussy's and Madame Sevigné's.' Being both gay and amusing is a hard act to pull off these days, but do at least try to include either some infor-mation which is newsworthy or some sentiment which is worth expressing.

5. Write in a natural manner

Don't think that putting your words on paper means you entirely have to alter how you express yourself. If you are not sure about what you want to put try saying it out loud first.

6. Sign off properly

Working out how to sign off is easy. Don't put 'Love' unless this is someone you do love. Generally it works like this:

- If you started 'Dear Mr Cicero,' then you finish with 'Yours sincerely'.

- If you began 'Dear Sir/Madam,' then end with 'Yours faithfully'.

- Generally, if you are replying, you should adopt a tone similar to the one in which you were addressed. So don't reply 'Dear Sir' to someone who began their letter 'Hi Mary'.

7. Make sure the envelope is legible

If you've spent half an hour writing a letter, it's probably worth taking the trouble to ensure that the Post Office can work out where to deliver it.

8. Put the right postage on

A letter which the recipient has had to pay for is never going to be quite as welcome as one that arrived for free.

Email

Computers in the future may weigh no more than 1.5 tons.

Popular Mechanics, 1949

The first email or electronic missive ever sent from one computer to another was a test message from US programmer Ray Tomlinson, sent in 1971 to a computer right next to him. It said something as insignificant as 'QWERTYUIOP'. It was Ray who came up with the idea of indicating separate computers by using the @ symbol. Some of that early history is recognised every day, as there are still an astonishing number of emails with insignificant content sent all the time. According to Radicati, a Californian technology research firm with nothing better to do, in 2013 approximately 507 billion email messages will be sent in the world each day. Almost everyone who has an email account feels bombarded, so …

1. Don't email because you don't want to say something in person

Bad news ought to be delivered in person. If you are breaking up with someone or firing them, you owe them enough respect not to do it by email. It's not fun but it's the right thing to do.

2. Make sure you have something to say

The clue is whether your words would be worth committing to paper. Is it important and if it is, might it be better said in person or on the phone?

3. Help the recipient by filling in the 'subject' field

It'll help them to know if the message is urgent or not and whether to delete it immediately or later. It also makes old emails easier to find. Then keep to the point. Wading through long emails is dull and life is short.

4. Write properly

Imagine you are writing a letter. Be polite, use whole sentences with punctuation, use upper- and lower-case letters but don't overuse CAPITAL LETTERS. IT LOOKS AS IF YOU ARE SHOUTING. The same goes for too many exclamation marks.

5. Make sure people included in group emails want to be in a group

You may be revealing someone's email address who wishes to stay anonymous. If you are trying to organise a group event, remember how annoying it can be for others to suddenly be on the receiving end of a lot of emails from people they don't know relating their diary availability.

6. Beware sarcasm

It never reads well in an email. Jokes can also be awkward. If someone keeps sending you 'hilarious' jokes and you don't want them, it is all right to gently suggest to the sender that perhaps they are not for you. Reading nuance and emotion in an email is not easy, but remember that emoticons can be trying.

7. Don't pass on chain letters

Don't even pass on virus warnings. These may well contain the virus itself.

8. Be careful what you forward

Cut and paste a message in case the original sender doesn't want their email address broadcast. There is no swifter way to harm a relationship than the misforwarded email. Passing on a virus because you couldn't be bothered to buy some security software is also not kind. Beware. You will almost certainly rue your own parsimony.

8b. Try to use words like 'parsimony'

Too many emails are so dull and badly written – and I don't just mean the ones from Nigerians with money transfer issues or Russian women with sex advice. The fact that these messages are sent and arrive quickly doesn't mean you can't take your time to write them well.

Orthography

Bad spelling is disgraceful, and many people spell badly from simple carelessness.

Collier's Cyclopaedia of Social and Commercial Information, 1882

That's spelling to you and me, but it's also punctuation and things like hyphens and capital letters. You don't have to send a properly constructed email but it says something about you if you don't.

In these days of spill and grummar check no email ought to suffer from these problems.

THE TELEPHONE

Middle age is when you're sitting at home on a Saturday night and the telephone rings and you hope it isn't for you.

Ogden Nash (1902–71), American poet

I once knew someone who required a psychiatric assessment. 'Do you ever hear voices when no one else is in the room?' asked the shrink earnestly. 'Yes,' said the fellow. The psychiatrist leant forward, 'When does this mainly occur?' she enquired. 'When I'm on the phone,' he replied.

The first telephone was patented by Alexander Graham Bell in 1876. It's worth bearing in mind that Bell himself found his new invention intrusive and refused to have one in his study. Telephones have changed shape and accessibility, but their basic use has remained the same.

Calling

1. Don't be cross if someone doesn't answer
It is almost too easy to get hold of people today. If they don't answer then allow for the fact that they may be busy.

2. Say who you are
'Hi, it's me' is a hopeless way of starting a conversation. Don't presume the person you are calling knows who it is. Not everyone sounds like themselves on the phone and, horror of horror, you may not sound that distinctive.

3. Don't hang up abruptly
It's a conversation. Make sure the other person has finished saying what they needed to.

Answering

1. Be clear and polite

Remember – you don't have to answer the phone so don't do it if you haven't got time to be polite.

2. Take a message

If the call is not for you, ask if the caller wants to leave a message. Make sure you write down any necessary details such as name and number to pass on to the person who missed the call. (I am mainly speaking now to you, Mary.)

3. Be nice to strangers

Even people who cold-call for a living are humans trying to earn a buck. Even those who are trying to obtain your bank details in order to rob you can be refused politely.

THE MOBILE PHONE

The first mobile phone call took place on 17 June 1946 inside a car installed with a phone in St Louis, Missouri. It would be more than a quarter of a century before you didn't need the car to make the call. The first handheld device used to ring someone was made by Motorola and the inaugural call took place on 3 April 1973. The phone weighed two and a half pounds and was nine inches long.

Today there are about 6 billion mobile phone subscriptions on a planet with about 7 billion people. Mobile devices have become an integral part of much of modern life. The important thing to remember is that a mobile phone is not an extension of your arm. You can put them down occasionally. You will feel naked but it's good for you.

There are also a few basics to bear in mind:

1. Consider your ringtone

These days you can programme your phone to have any ringtone you want. You can even record yourself and make your own text alerts. Much like your Avatar on Twitter, your ringtone says a lot about who you are. If you want 'Bring your Daughter to the Slaughter' blasting out in the middle of a meeting, then good for you. If, of course, you haven't wondered if this is appropriate then you may have a lot of time to do so when you're fired.

2. Don't shout

It's a phone. It has a tremendously sensitive transmitter designed to carry the sound of your voice without you needing to shout. Consider your volume levels. There is little more awkward than a bus full of passengers listening to one woman's fight for sexual liberation. Always remember that you have the option of carrying on the conversation at home. In private.

If someone asks you to be quieter in a public space, know that you were too loud. Respect the courage it took to ask you in the first place.

3. Never put your phone on speaker in public

No one wants to hear your conversation. It's rude, it's unnecessary and it's plain stupid. If you are too exhausted to hold a phone to your ear, get a Bluetooth headset or maybe write a letter.

4. Turn your phone off when meeting someone

If you are meeting someone in person give them your full attention. Turn your phone off. Put it away. It's OK. It'll still be there in half an hour.

5. Turn your phone off during dinner

See general notes on table manners.

6. Turn your phone off in the theatre/cinema/ other public space

No one wants to reach the emotional climax of a film only to have the 'goosebumps' moment ruined by the buzzing of a phone. You also don't need to check who has 'liked' you on Facebook. Most films are only ninety minutes. A play often has an interval. You can last until then. Really you can.

7. Turn your phone off for romance

I won't go into details. Unless you are determinedly single you will know why.

8. Don't use the phone in a queue

Multi-tasking is a wonderful talent, but manners are just as important. If you're in a shop and ordering a coffee for example, it's always nice if you pay attention to the person serving you. If you're jabbering away on the phone whilst someone is trying to do their job, don't be surprised if the quality of service you receive is poor.

9. Never use your phone in the 'Quiet' carriage on a train

The clue is in the word 'quiet'. It is really all right to ask someone to respect this if you do it calmly and politely. Do it at the time. Don't wait until the train pulls in at its destination, you are spluttering with rage and it's too late for the offenders to do anything about it. I was once on a train with the Australian writer Clive James. At a stop a young man got on dressed from head to toe in camouflage gear. Clive looked at him and said, 'I do hope you're not coming on here to be weird.' The man left immediately.

10. Don't ever answer or make a call from the bathroom

It's just wrong.

Texting

The single biggest problem in communication is the illusion that it has taken place.

George Bernard Shaw (1856–1950), playwright

These days the telephone is not just the modern equivalent of two tin cans and piece of string for joining distant voices. It can be used as a multi-functional port of call for many kinds of interaction. Typed messages used to be sent by telex and the sound of my father's machine rattling in the night as messages passed from Europe to the US is part of my childhood soundtrack. The first SMS message in the world was sent on 3 December 1992 when an engineer called Neil Papworth texted the words 'Merry Christmas' to his friend Richard. I don't know how many messages are sent each day now. More than 6 billion I think. If I find out I'll text you.

These days we are bombarded with communication and a lot of it is unnecessary. I like the well-known rule about texting – **WAIT**. Which stands for ...

Why
Am
I
Texting ?

I'd add to that:

1. Check the time
Just because you are in a bar and awake doesn't mean everyone else is. Don't assume that you can text at any time.

2. Dnt txt spk
What makes you so busy? Write in full sentences. There is always time for vowels but at the same time ...

3. Don't text whole novels
A rough guide is that anything over 140 characters deserves to go in an email or, even better, a phone call.

4. Don't text pictures of yourself in any compromising situations
It'll come back to haunt you. Maybe not today, maybe not tomorrow, but soon. And for the rest of your life. In order to avoid this ...

5. Don't send messages when you are emotional or drunk or both

You will live in the land of regret.

6. Don't text life-changing messages

Texting is not for breaking up with someone or telling them out of the blue that someone they know has passed away. While you're not upsetting someone, also …

7. Take the time to make sure that you send your text message to the right person

Many a friendship and relationship has fallen foul of such an easy technological faux pas.

8. Unless you know them well, don't presume the person you are texting will know who you are

Sign a text so the recipient is very clear who it has come from or the message is pointless. Don't presume you are so important that they have kept you in their contacts list. If someone texts you by mistake – text back to let them know. It may be life changing for someone.

SOCIAL MEDIA

Here is where I probably begin to sound like someone disinclined to embrace the modern way. On the surface, social media is a marvellous new way for people to stay in touch but a lot of its use reminds me of the story about …

The Tower of Babel

According to the Bible there was a time when 'the whole earth was of one language, and of one speech' and all the people on earth got together to build a tower that would reach all the way to heaven. Apparently God didn't like this and he said:

> Behold, the people is one, and they have all one language; and this they begin to do: and now nothing will be restrained from them, which they have imagined to do. Go to, let us go down, and there confound their language, that they may not understand one another's speech.

After that he scattered all the people all over the earth and made everyone speak in different languages so they could never again decide to build such a tower. The tower was known as Babel and it's a story which you find in one form or another throughout history. There are Jewish versions of the story, Hindu, Armenian, Estonian and so on. With so many cultures repeating the story about the dangers of global communication it might be worth a passing thought.

Hello everyone!

It took Facebook ten months to go from a million users to 5 million. Now there are a billion users, about 500 million people on Twitter, of whom 200 million are active users, and approximately 4 billion videos are viewed on YouTube every day. The person with the most Twitter followers is Lady Gaga, with 33,060,527 having hooked up to her pronouncements. She is ahead of Justin Bieber, Katy Perry and Rihanna, with Barack Obama in fifth place. The fact is, there are 7,157,978 people in the world more interested in finding out what Justin Bieber thinks than in following the president of the United States.

Free speech is a wonderful thing and it has been hard fought for. It was in 1964 that a student of the University of California called Jack Weinberg was distributing leaflets on the Berkeley campus promoting civil rights. The university banned on-campus political activities and, though it's hard to believe, a police car arrived with the police ready to arrest him. In an early example of a flash mob, about 3,000 of Weinberg's fellow students decided to sit down around the police vehicle and refused to move. The stand-off lasted for thirty-two hours, with students using the car as a speaker's podium. The charges against Weinberg were eventually dropped.

There is much to commend the democratisation of communication, but it strikes me as a system which is fraught with possible difficulties. If you applaud free speech (which you should), you need to bear in mind that it means other people are also free to say what they like. This may include the unpalatable. Twitter is a very good example of what happens if there are no set manners to control human behaviour. It is worth bearing in mind that these forms of communication are not very old. Perhaps it will all settle down and the things that Twitter is currently going through will turn out to be a sort of technological teenagehood of bad behaviour. One can only hope.

As well, however, as unleashing the dogs of suspect dogma and the poodles of prejudice, sadly, much social media is used to help create a notion that someone is a ...

Celebrity

It is not uncommon to measure someone's fame by the number of people who hang on their every word on Twitter or befriend them on Facebook. At one time, such a desperate desire to be the focus of everyone's attention would have been seen as – and here is a word you never hear any more – vulgar. Seeking fame for its own sake rather than having it seek you for some achievement or other is something modern media has made possible. It carries its own risks. Some celebrities who were once addicted to Twitter, like the actor Ashton Kutcher, have been burned by the experience and have handed control of their accounts to management companies. Fame has always been a two-edged sword. It was in around 620 BC that an Athenian law-maker called Draco, whilst attending theatre on the island of Aegina, was smothered to death by gifts of cloaks showered upon him by appreciative citizens.

I am not a fan of the idea of pursuing fame for its own sake. I think the genius animator Walt Disney had it about right when he explained what it was like to be a celebrity. 'It feels fine,' he explained, 'when it helps to get a good seat for a football game. But it never helped me to make a good film or a good shot in a polo game, or command the obedience of my daughter. It doesn't even seem to keep fleas off our dogs – and if being a celebrity won't give one an advantage over a couple of fleas, then I guess there can't be much in being a celebrity after all.'

If you wish to reveal your innermost thoughts to absolutely anyone on the planet with the press of a few buttons then it's probably worth having a think about a few possible guidelines first.

General online behaviour or watching your gob

There is a sense of distance about online communication which makes people think they can behave badly. Take the person who gives an author a one-star review for their book even though they haven't actually read it. The person who grumpily slams a bed and breakfast under a pseudonym because they had a disappointing weekend which was really nothing to do with the standard of accommodation. Nowhere has this kind of thoughtless and sometimes unkind behaviour been made more apparent than on …

Twitter

This is an information network. Anyone can write a very small blog at any time. It should be very simple. You have 140 characters in each message with which to express yourself and it can take less than that to ruin your life.

When former New York Representative, Anthony Weiner, sent a twenty-four-character tweet linked to a picture of a bulge in a pair of men's underpants, it ended his career. This is not just the modern system for sending the equivalent of a telegram; it is also a giant game of *Chinese Whispers*, *Scrabble* and *Risk* all wrapped into one.

Twitter language: Tweet

Twitter is like standing at a bus stop and shouting what you think except everyone can hear you and you can never take it back. Even if you delete a tweet it's still out there in cyberspace. Twitter is something that can be done on the run and that is one of the pitfalls. That can lead to mistakes. Think carefully about who you want to share information with, so it's probably best not to do it when angry, drunk or both. If you have a tendency to let loose late at night, find somewhere to hide your phone from yourself, like a plastic bag at the bottom of a lake. Follow some simple rules:

1. Try to be interesting

Beware the needy devil that is narcissism. Tweeting details about your life such as 'I'm having toast' or 'I'm off to bed' is of no interest to anyone. There are about 400 million tweets a day. Does the world really need to know more about you? You are taking up that most precious commodity – time; yours and everyone else's.

2. Be yourself

If you claim you are Angelina Jolie but are in fact a carpet fitter from Nottingham called Nigel, someone will find out.

3. Be pleasant

Don't spend all your time pointing out other people's mistakes. You are likely to make some of your own. If you wouldn't say what you've tweeted to someone's face, don't say it on Twitter. Be careful not to tweet how bored you are at a meeting or party whilst you're at the event. You are not the only person on Twitter and someone in the room with you may see it.

4. Do beware showing off

Sometimes people who are 'following' you recommend you to others. This is called 'Follow Friday' or #FF. If you get #FF's be pleased! But be pleased within yourself. Don't tell everyone. Arrogance is always unattractive.

5. Think of your own jokes

Here is your chance to express yourself and bear in mind that famous comedians will get quite cross if you steal their material. They probably have millions of followers and could easily rustle up an online lynch mob. (This is like an actual lynch mob but with fewer horses.)

6. Make sure you are on sure ground with a political rant

Have a think before you tweet a knee-jerk reaction to something. Hard to believe but you may not have all the facts.

7. Don't pass on gossip

Those who tweeted allegations against the Tory peer, Lord McAlpine, when they mistakenly thought he was involved in a sex scandal, later had to consult their lawyers.

8. Don't be a troll or feed one

It's curious how the most modern of media harks back to mythology. Unkind folk on social media are known as 'trolls'. In my Scandinavian childhood these were ugly little men who hid under bridges and tried to steal your goat. The best advice is quite simply 'don't feed the trolls'. Take the moral high ground and don't engage. If someone insults you, deal with it with dignity. Don't start a slanging match. Use the social media equivalent of the eject button in a James Bond car. The 'Block button' enables you essentially to erase the insulting party from your online life.

Putting 'LOL' or a smiley face at the end of a nasty tweet doesn't lessen the damage it might do. Pick up some knitting. Work for a charity. Bake some scones. There's a whole world out there to enjoy.

9. Try not to look desperate or weird

Just because you follow someone on Twitter does not mean you know them. Celebrities are easily frightened away from Twitter, so berating them if they don't reply to your specific critique of their work is unnecessary. It's tough, but try to treat them as if they're human beings. 'Followers' are not like the ones Jesus had. They don't actually care about you. If you spend all your time tweeting you won't have a life. Step away from your computer or you'll never have anything worth tweeting about.

10. Do let people know about funny videos of pandas sneezing

Twitter lurking

Some people have a Twitter account but don't tweet. They use their account in order to join the system and let them see others' tweets. This is not that far off listening behind someone's door. If you meet someone whose tweets you've been watching, try not to reveal the fact that you know their every move. It's one move away from stalking. Bizarrely, I have a Twitter account but neither tweet nor look at what is being tweeted. I have the account simply to stop others impersonating me – which has actually been happening. What a strange world it is.

Swearing on Twitter

See the general section on swearing. It's the same however you communicate.

Facebook

Facebook is a social networking service. It was founded in 2004 but you may already know this as there was quite a big movie about it. Almost as soon as it became successful its founders had the bad manners to start suing each other. One might call it the Babel Effect. The original intention behind the service was to enable students at Harvard to compare photos of other students and decide who was 'hottest'. It has grown into a rather more commercial site where anyone can tell the world about them- selves. You'd think this would be simple but, like Twitter, this new world has its own rules, too.

1. Don't boast about how many friends you have on Facebook

In order to be in touch with someone on Facebook you have to 'friend' them. To put it kindly – this is misleading. Most people on Facebook are not your friends. You will never meet them, you will never go on holiday with them. If you see the number of Facebook 'friends' as a sort of popularity contest then you need to get out more.

According to evolutionary psychologist Professor Robin Dunbar of Oxford University we can amass as many thousands of friends on Facebook as we like but that doesn't alter human beings' ability in reality to have only about 150 real friends.

2. Don't update your 'Facebook status' when you are drunk

You may put something you regret or insult someone. Don't 'unfriend' someone because the demon drink is playing havoc with your synapses. You will have to explain yourself in the morning.

3. Be careful what you 'like'

When you post a status update your 'friends' have the option to 'like' it. Some people will 'like' everything that you post. Be careful not to 'like' the wrong things. For example, if someone lets you know that it's the anniversary of a family member's death, that would not be a thing to 'like'.

Don't 'like' your own updates. That's just weird.

4. Don't attention seek

If you post things like 'Sarah has never felt so alone … ' in order to get the attention you never got as a child, you should perhaps befriend your GP.

5. Don't be desperate

Don't bombard people you don't know with messages and 'friend' requests. If you don't know them in real life why are you bothered? It's like asking Meryl Streep to come to your office Christmas party and getting angry when she doesn't show up.

6. Be careful about jokes

You might find a video which you post of a cat dressed as Margaret Thatcher very amusing but your friend might not. Many work-places now police their employees' social media presence. Try not to get someone fired for the sake of a cheap laugh. You can put NSFW next to something to indicate it is Not Suitable / Safe for Work, meaning open this somewhere else, you fool. Also bear in mind that 'frape', the act of raping someone else's Facebook profile while they are logged on, can be hilarious or disastrous. Your call.

7. Don't ruin someone else's life

Everyone likes an amusing photo, but not everyone likes having an amusing photo of themselves put on Facebook. If you've taken a snap late at night in a strip club of your married male friend 'getting to know' a woman who is not his wife, do not use the much abused 'tagging' facility. This allows you to name the people in the photograph and automatically posts it on their wall. Again, do something else. How are those scones getting on?

8. Don't ruin your own life

If you have phoned in sick, called off a date or made any form of excuse, make sure you don't ruin it by posting 'having fun getting drunk on a paddle steamer'. You will get found out. Also bear in mind that what you post online about your holiday exploits will come back to haunt you. Are you sure you want those pictures made public?

9. Beware 'humble brags'

That's the act of pretending to be humble whilst actually telling your 'friends' how amazing you are. Such updates usually start 'Apparently I'm …'. For example, 'Apparently I'm being promoted to the head of the company!'. Conversely, make sure you don't make things up such as 'I've been scouted by an international model agency!'. When you turn up for work on Monday morning as usual you'll just look silly.

10. Face reality

Just to reiterate – these are almost certainly not your real friends. If someone says something horrible, unless it is of a criminal nature, leave it alone.

A note on friendship

Piglet sidled up to Pooh from behind. 'Pooh?' he whispered.

'Yes, Piglet?'

'Nothing,' said Piglet, taking Pooh's hand. 'I just wanted to be sure of you.'

A. A. Milne, *Winnie-the-Pooh*

Ideally friends have more things in common than an obsessive desire to amass strangers' names on their social media pages. Good friends are invaluable and have mutual affection and respect for each other. Think Thelma and Louise, Han Solo and Chewbacca or Butch Cassidy and the Sundance Kid. The word comes from the Old English word *freond* meaning to love or favour. Friends are great because, unlike relatives, you can choose them. I have a wonderful group of friends and think of them like wagons circling around me whenever I feel under attack by the world.

When I was a child I never understood what the phrase having to 'work at relationships' meant. Now I know that it means if you don't make time for people, you may find they've moved on without you realising. So here's a few tips on friendship:

1. Be loyal

If you are a good friend to someone then you shouldn't want to gossip about them behind their back.

2. Be cheerful

It's just as easy as being grumpy and much nicer for your pals. Don't be the whiner that no one wants to have wine with. If you smile as a default position you quite quickly get used to it.

3. Be careful about borrowing

Borrowing money is a quick route to trouble between friends. Borrowing clothing is fine, but if you keep borrowing the same item then maybe it's something you need to go and buy for yourself.

4. Stick to plans if you can

Everyone's time is valuable. If you keep cancelling arrangements it suggests you haven't got time for someone.

5. Be honest

If you are upset about something it is better to say so and clear the air. If you feel used or misused by a friend, tell them, and see if you can sort things out before it gets ugly and you've said bad things about them on Facebook. Honest advice is what friends are for. Try giving and taking it in a constructive spirit.

6. Don't be a doormat

Friendship is not a master-servant relationship. It is supposed to be a two-way street. If it isn't, find a new friend. If you're always the butt of the joke get your butt out of there.

That was a lot of words. Let me try to summarise it for you in 140 characters.

My dear Mary

Communication between people is a splendid thing.
It can make your heart sing.
Think, listen and be kind
and if someone is dull
do try not to mind.

Time now, I think, to head out and about and meet some people in the flesh.

Much love

Sandi

5: OUT AND ABOUT

When in Company, put not your Hands to any Part of the Body, not usualy Discovered.

George Washington, First President of the United States
Rules of Civility & Decent Behaviour In Company and Conversation

Dear Mary

It's the big one – the grand circle of existence. You know how to behave at home, how to eat without causing others distress, the basics of how to communicate – you are ready for the wider world, the world that includes complete strangers.

Let's take a look at the fundamentals of being out and about in public places. Some of this may seem a little obvious but you would be surprised how often you see people blithely ignoring the fundamentals. That 'rule' quoted above was written by George Washington when he was just sixteen. It's tempting to think he must have been quite a prissy lad to be so concerned with 'Decent Behaviour' at that age but perhaps that's the sort of quality you need in a future leader. He was right, of course. Boys in particular seem to find it difficult not to rummage about with their private parts, even in public, so they need reminding:

1. Leave your tackle alone when you are with other people

It's partly a hygiene thing – no one wants to know where those hands have been and it's partly a sense of respect for others. Focus on the beauty around you, with your present company, rather than fussing about with your genitalia which will still be there when you get home. You will also need your hands to ...

2. Open doors for others

This one has caused a slight stir in the past. I don't know who invented the door. We still say 'open *up*' in relation to doors, presumably because somewhere in our historic DNA we recall pushing up the flap of a tent. I suspect the person we should really thank is the one who invented the door knob. Traditionally it used to be men who opened doors for women. This may have arisen from the heavy floor-length garments that women wore in medieval times, although I can't imagine it was easy clanking through in armour either. These days, I think opening a door for someone else is non-gender specific. The fact is, being polite never hurt anyone. You can both be solicitous about each other's comfort. It's about reading the moment and responding with sensitivity. Sometimes the dynamic is very clear and at other times you need to get to know each other better. If you are going through a public door, check to see if there is anyone behind you who you might help. An older person or someone with a buggy may be glad of the help.

3. Spitting in public

Don't. Ancient Roman women used to spit down the front of their dresses to ward off the evil eye. This is no longer necessary.

4. Anything to do with mucus

I don't need to say it, right? Don't pick your nose, don't blow it on your sleeve ... For some reason putting your tongue to the roof of your mouth helps ward off sneezing, temporarily at least.

5. Focus

If you do meet someone unexpectedly, take a moment to pay attention to them. Do not text, consult your watch or in any way indicate you wish you were somewhere else. If you really are in a hurry, say so and arrange another time to meet up.

GREETINGS

Shaking hands

There was a time when only men shook hands and they did it to show they didn't intend to kill the person being greeted. Proffering your empty hand proves you are not carrying a sword or dagger with which to do anyone any harm. These leftovers of knightly behaviour used also to be echoed in men tipping or lifting their hats in greeting, just as a knight in armour might have lifted his visor to reveal his face.

Shaking hands is still polite, although on the whole it seems to remain a predominantly male to male activity. In business, women do now offer their hands to be shaken. It is nice to offer a firm handshake. There is nothing worse than a grip like wet lettuce, but it is equally hideous to crush someone's fingers with your enthusiasm.

Greeting with a kiss

Kissing is the bit where someone puts their lips on a part of someone else's body. It can be done for lots of reasons – to say hello in a more intimate manner than handshaking, to say you like someone (granny, lover, child, etc.), to be polite or even for political reasons. People have been kissing since lips were invented and it's a pleasurable business. Welcome kisses, particularly romantic ones, release a chemical called dopamine into your system which makes you feel utterly splendid.

Using a kiss as a greeting is more prevalent in some cultures than others, so you need to be at your most sensitive if you are not sure. On the whole, the kiss used in a greeting is planted on the cheek not the lips. If you are not sure, aim for the cheek. It is fine to just brush your cheek against someone else's and certainly the full smack of your lips on their face is never required. The number of kisses varies from culture to culture and in some places from neighbourhood to neighbourhood. There are rural parts of the United States where cheek kissing is seen as horribly pretentious while in some cities it is considered the norm. Take your time. Watch what indicators the other person is giving as they approach you. If you both pay attention to the greeting, then you will silently know which cheek is being offered and how many kisses are required. There isn't one rule. There is only sensitivity. (Check your Top Cs again.) If you feel a need to control the situation, as you shake hands place your left hand on the arm of the person you are greeting and move your head to the left to indicate that you intend to kiss them on the right cheek. Removing your hand from their arm will hopefully indicate that the greeting is over.

If you are travelling abroad, you should read up on the accepted rules for the particular area where you are spending time. In general, men should not kiss a woman who they are meeting for the first time at all. Men should, however, be prepared to kiss other men in countries such as Turkey, but again, not at a first meeting.

MANNERS ON THE STREET

In a large town and in busy thoroughfares the gentleman should offer his arm; but in the country this is not allowable.

Eliza Cheadle, *Manners of Modern Society*, 1872

There was a time when roads consisted entirely of pavement. This was before the invention of the wheel when roads weren't much to write home about. Indeed, writing home wasn't much to write home about. When the Romans first arrived in Britain they probably weren't all that impressed with the road system. They went on to build more than 2,000 miles of very straight road so that they could get about the place.

Something to write home about

Interestingly, the Romans did write home. The *Vindolanda* tablets found at Hadrian's Wall consist of handwritten letters to the garrison. The soldiers write about underwear and extra socks and one of the most famous documents was written by Claudia Severa, the wife of the commander of a nearby fort, in conjunction with one of her servants. It was an invitation to Sulpicia Lepidina, inviting her to a birthday party in AD 100. I like to think it was sent in plenty of time and with proper RSVP instructions.

Pavements were invented when people started driving too fast and pedestrians decided they wanted to stay alive.

The Victorians had many rules about how pedestrians should conduct themselves which involved women not walking too fast, gentlemen carrying parcels and a general ban on eating. We don't have quite so many rules today but there are still a few.

1. Dress appropriately

You can wear a bikini in the high street but only if you really want to draw attention to yourself. Knowing what is the correct attire for any public appearance has a lot to do with cultural context. There is the story of Jean Jules Jusserand, who for twenty-three years was France's ambassador to Washington. He served through four presidential administrations and was a confidant of President Roosevelt. Jusserand was a dapper fellow and one day he and the president were out for a walk. The debonair Frenchman sported an afternoon suit, top hat and kid gloves, while the president was more casually attired in rough tweed and rugged boots. Roosevelt liked to think of himself as an outdoorsman and he bounded out into the country. When they arrived at a deep stream, the president insisted they take their clothes off and swim across. The ambassador did as he was told but he kept his gloves on. 'Otherwise,' he apparently declared, 'it would be embarrassing if we should meet any ladies.'

2. If you meet someone, don't stand and chat in the middle of the pavement

It's exceptionally rare to have a street to yourself. The trouble with public places is that they are full of the public. If you want to chat rather than process, move to one side. Others may have places to get to and you are in the way. The worst-case scenario is that they will step into the road to get round you and be hit by moving traffic.

3. Don't walk in a great gang

People walking in groups tend to walk more slowly, so you will both block the pavement and be annoying.

4. Protect the old and the young

If you are walking with someone, bear in mind that the safest part of the pavement is the section away from the road. When walking with the very young or the very old, place them on the inside of the pavement nearest any buildings.

5. Use your eyes

It's usually not that difficult to see another person. Some of them are quite big. If birds can fly in formation without hitting each other, we ought to be able to navigate a bit of sidewalk. It helps not to text while you walk. If you do bump into someone say 'sorry'.

6. Don't drop litter

If everyone did, then you wouldn't be able to use the pavement. If you see someone littering, the best thing is to point to the offending article and say 'I think you dropped something'. Most people are embarrassed enough to pick it up again.

7. Consider the zebra

Zebra crossings exist to make the whole interaction of pedestrian with motorised vehicles safer. They were introduced to the UK in 1949 and were originally blue and yellow. There are a few tips for their use which make life easier for everyone.

- Don't approach the crossing from a diagonal on the pavement. Stand at one end and give drivers a chance to stop. This is not a brake test.

- Don't stand chatting at the end of a crossing so that car drivers keep thinking you want to cross and slow down.

- Say thank you or wave or do something indicating gratitude if someone stops and lets you across.

8. Eating while walking

Try not to. It's a quick route to indigestion. You won't enjoy the food and no one will enjoy watching you.

PUBLIC TRANSPORT - TRAINS AND BUSES

A private railroad car is not an acquired taste. One takes to it immediately.

Eleanor Robson Belmont (1879–1979),
English actress and Broadway star

Trains are one of the places most complained about in terms of bad manners. In fact in 2012 the 25 per cent increase in complaints about rudeness on the French national railway, SNCF, led the train company to employ 2,700 inspectors with the power to fine people for all manner of misdemeanours from smoking to putting their feet on the seat. I suspect that buses, too, have their fair share of passengers with irritating traits.

1. Stay positive

If the train or bus is delayed, try to stay positive. Nothing makes a long journey more awkward than someone losing control and screaming blue murder. No one will ever join in. It's not *Braveheart*.

2. Watch your space

If you're in a double seat be aware of your fellow passenger's body. The armrest is in place to constrain you, not to indicate where you should be spilling over. Try to ascertain where the lines are. The middle of the table on a train, for example, marks the furthest that your feet should reach.

If there are lots of empty seats on a carriage, sit in one that's not beside a fellow passenger. It's always a bit off when someone sits right beside you on a bus that's empty apart from you. Weird and uncomfortable.

If the train or bus is crowded and you see someone standing who is older than you, more infirm or more pregnant, let them sit down. Someday you may be old, infirm … the pregnant thing rather depends on your gender.

3. Mind your stuff

Why put your bag in the luggage rack when you can place it handily in the aisles? You don't need an answer, do you? If you are short ask someone taller to assist you in placing your belongings safely away from harm.

4. Mind your meals

No one wants to sit opposite someone eating six cheeseburgers and a bucket of chicken. Be considerate about mess and smells. Some food smells more than others. You're in a closed compartment. Consider other people's noses.

5. Keep cleaning to yourself

Public transport is not the place to exercise your cleaning routine with people around you. Don't treat the train or bus as if it is your front room. Exercise some boundaries. No one wants to share your nail parings, excess hair or watch you clean your teeth.

6. Don't put your feet on the seat

Why not? Because someone will have to sit there and get the muck from your shoes on their clothes.

7. Don't bring livestock

OK, this is really unlikely but I once had a very bad journey with a chicken. If you do have a pet with you – keep it with you. Your fellow passengers joined a train (or bus), not a petting zoo.

8. Know your stop

Have a rough idea when you are due in at your station or stop so that you have time to gather your things together calmly. If you rush you are bound to trip over someone and hit them with your bag.

QUIET!

There are a few things here. The first is ...

Type quietly

This may just be me but it's my book and I've been trying to be helpful for ages so cut me some slack. I understand that some people need to work on the train. I don't understand why typing needs to be so loud. It's mostly men, I'm afraid. They bash the keyboard as if it were some wild beast which will only do their bidding if it is subdued first. Allow me an aside to those men – Fellows! It's an inanimate object! It's not going anywhere. It will work just as well if you are gentle ... and quiet.

Turn the phone off

No phone works well on any train anywhere. You will end up shouting. Please don't. You would be amazed at what you can accomplish with a silent text message instead. If someone else is shouting, there is probably nothing you can do about it. Trains and buses are not good places to start a row. The best thing is to move seats.

Mind electronic noise

Portable DVD players, games, anything that makes a noise needs to be used so as not to annoy fellow passengers. Unless you are royalty you are unlikely to have the carriage to yourself. If you have kids and they have anything portable which makes a noise, make sure that it can either be muted or that they have headphones. They may be enjoying something tuneful from Disney or be thrilled with the variety of beeping sounds their electronic game can make but the other passengers may want to kill them.

On a train, the quiet coach is serious business. Depending on the other passengers, 'quiet' can mean 'don't breathe'. Even the act of eating a packet of crisps can result in the police being called. Only sit in the quiet coach if you are sure that you can sit quietly without moving for the duration of your journey.

RULES FOR MOTORISTS

Money may not buy happiness, but I'd rather cry in a Jaguar than on a bus.

Françoise Sagan (1935–2004), French writer

When I bought my first car for £400 I phoned my father in great excitement. 'What kind is it?' he enquired. 'A yellow one' I replied.

Driving is awash with rules which have the might of the law behind them. These are helpfully compiled in a bestselling book called *The Highway Code* which has been available since 1931. Oddly, this still doesn't mean that all drivers comply with them. Even the calmest person can suffer from 'road rage' if they perceive that another driver has not behaved well. Road rage can be a problem as the person in a rage is also in charge of half a ton of metal travelling at speed. The best thing is to avoid this kind of explosive fury.

1. Follow the rules of the road
They are for everyone. When you are driving there is nothing special about you.

2. Have some idea where you are going

Nothing is more infuriating than the person who hesitates or is in the wrong lane. If you are not sure, find a safe place to pull over and ask or look at a map.

3. Be patient with the person who has no idea where he is going

It could be you next time. Over-zealous horn beeping is only acceptable in Road Runner cartoons and indeed is now outlawed in some cities.

4. Indicate

Here I am going to sound like a grumpy old person so be prepared. The indicator seems to be the one part of a car which is now treated as an optional extra. Indicating at roundabouts or indicating at all seems to have gone out of fashion. If you are steering half a ton of metal, it is kind to other drivers, bicyclists and even pedestrians to let the world know where you are thinking of heading.

5. Say thank you

If other drivers let you into their lane or the stream of traffic say thank you with a wave, a thumbs up or some other gesture of cheer.

6. Don't use your phone

It's against the law and it's dangerous. Don't text or chat or set your satnav while you are supposed to be concentrating on driving. There are plenty of examples of people texting 'See you later' while driving off a bridge.

7. Park prettily

I once saw a sign requesting that I 'Park Prettily'. I wasn't entirely sure what it meant but I suspect abandoning your car across several spaces so no one else can park would not comply.

IF YOU DON'T HAVE A CAR

1. Getting picked up

Never make the person who is picking you up wait. This includes your parents. Don't take your time even though the very very nice person says they are OK to wait in the car. This includes your parents.

If you want a lift home, ask nicely and well in advance. Don't simply follow the driver to their car. Be accommodating about where you could be dropped. Don't expect it to be a door-to-door cab service and don't hold the driver up by spending hours saying goodbye.

2. Be a clean passenger

Make sure your shoes are clean and you are not wiping dirt all over the mats. Don't eat in the car. Be careful not to leave your stuff behind. I won't say don't leave food wrappers because you shouldn't have been eating in the car in the first place. You don't want to give any more trouble to the person who literally went out of their way to pick you up.

3. Don't criticise their driving

It's a bit like kissing. Everyone has a sense they are quite good at it. Hardly anyone thinks they are a bad driver. If someone is driving badly, try not to cling on to the door or take sharp breaths every time another car approaches. It's not likely to help them drive any better. If necessary shut your eyes.

4. Repay favours

If the person repeatedly gives you a lift, offer to pay back in little ways such as buying coffee, or paying for parking or a toll. Offer, even if you know the driver won't accept. This includes your parents.

PLACES TO GO

Right, let's go and explore the world, even if some of it is a tad mind-numbing.

The supermarket

If you don't like supermarkets then blame Clarence Saunders, who opened the first self-service grocery shop called the Piggly Wiggly store in 1916 in Memphis, Tennessee. Today about 75 per cent of our food is bought from supermarkets so they are busy places and Saunders has a lot to answer for.

1. Do have trolley manners

However complex your yoghurt selection may be, and however much time you need to make it, there is no need to get in the way of the more decisive shopper. Don't abandon your trolley in the middle of an aisle to annoy everyone.

2. Trolley rage

It does happen. People can become enraged whilst wheeling a trolley. If someone has a problem with you, do not shout. Call for a member of staff.

3. Don't block the aisle with your social scene

It's the same as pavements – don't get in everyone's way just because you've bumped into someone. If you are shopping with your family don't stand discussing prospective meals so that no one else can get to the food. If someone else is in your way don't make a scene. It's just shopping, not a Mexican stand-off.

4. Don't squeeze everything

No one wants your hands all over the fresh fruit or bread.

5. Read the signs

You will upset people if you enter the 'Five items or less' or 'Basket only' queue and aren't eligible. In fact the degree of upset may be faintly astonishing. If you see someone with six items in the five items only aisle again, it's not worth duelling over. Actually, while we are waiting, let's consider the thorny issue of queuing for a moment.

Queuing

An Englishman, even if he is alone, forms an orderly queue of one.

George Mikes (1912–87), Hungarian-born British author

No race on earth seems to queue quite like the British. There seems to be an ingrained mechanism of patience for this form of waiting. George Mikes in his 1946 publication *How to be an Alien*, called it 'the national passion of an otherwise dispassionate race'. The next time you have to queue, and it's bound to come up (usually in the rain) consider its knightly origins. The word is fifteenth century and is not British at all but French for 'a tail' or, more impressively, the heraldic term 'tail of a beast'. This seems appropriate, as the first queue I can think of in history is when Noah managed to persuade all those animals to line up for a cruise. Some people see the ability to queue as a mark of British good manners, but the fact is, hard as it may be to believe, other nations also queue. The Danes have a very rigorous system of numbered tickets in every chemist to ensure that both the fit and the poorly are treated with equanimity.

Queuing is tedious but it's an equal opportunity employer. It's tedious for everyone. No one likes to queue. There is no one that I have ever met who regards queuing as a joyful occupation. It is basically a test to see how long you can stand in one place without beginning to either dribble or speak to yourself. There is nothing tempting about the 'dole queue'. Winston Churchill even invented the word 'Queuetopia' to warn Britain that under the Opposition they might be transformed into a socialist country in which people were required to queue for everything.

Self-service counters were invented in supermarkets to make people feel as though they were not queuing. In fact, by the time you have called six times for assistance at a self-service till, it has taken longer than waiting in line for someone to take the money from you. All queuing etiquette springs from a universal loathing of standing behind someone else. The electronic signs which call people forward in petrol stations and post offices were designed to make everyone feel that the system was 'fair' and that no one was queuing longer than anyone else.

There are some basic rules:

1. Jumping ahead in a queue
You will upset someone. Guaranteed.

2. If you need to leave a queue
You do have to ask someone to keep your place for you.

3. If someone pushes in to a queue
You can politely point out that there are people ahead of them. If you are in a queue of English people you are unlikely to need to do this as someone else will have already made their displeasure clear.

4. Joining a friend in a queue
This is allowable but it is still best to ask the person directly behind them if they mind. Having several friends join you is never going to be popular.

5. Try and resist the temptation to chat
Most people are too grumpy in a queue to want to make friends.

6. Watch your space
There is no need to breathe all over the person in front. They would be quicker if it were possible. Give them room to be grumpy.

7. Keep the kids corralled
Again, let's not add to the tension by allowing the children to run amok.

8. Be patient

It's a queue.

Theatre

One Christmas a friend gave my family tickets to see *The Nutcracker* at the Coliseum theatre in London. My daughters, then aged seven and nine, were thrilled. My son, Theo, who was three, was less impressed even though we were seated in the royal box. He wanted to play in the corridor with his car. 'Sit on my lap,' I cajoled. 'You might like the show.' He sat fidgeting but quietened as the house lights dimmed and the curtain went up. The stage began to fill with dancing toys and he seemed happy enough. The first scene finished and the stage darkened. It was as the lights came back up that I think Theo realised there was more to come. 'Oh, now what?' he said, loudly enough for the entire audience to hear and so full of *Weltschmerz* that a laugh echoed around the building. We went out into the corridor to play with his car.

The first rule of theatre is:

1. Don't be late

Theatre shows are always very clear about what time they are going to start. The management rather helpfully print it on the ticket. This is so that everyone can sit down together and not disturb each other by wandering in late and blocking the view. The performers will have rehearsed the show right from the beginning, not just the bit that starts ten minutes in. It would be nice to see it.

2. Be quiet

You are not on show, the actors are. If you hate the show it is quite possible that you may be alone in your opinion. Everyone in the audience is having their own reaction to the performance. If you really don't like what you are watching, keep that to yourself. Do not sigh, fidget, groan. The actors are no doubt doing their best. They have probably worked very hard. The fact that it is not working for you doesn't mean you shouldn't give them a chance to do their best. Perhaps you need to pay a bit more attention. If you really can't bear the performance, wait patiently and then leave quietly in the interval. I have sat through many public performances where I was not engaged in the slightest. I find those moments an excellent time to solve a knotty problem or compose a mental shopping list.

3. Turn off your mobile phone

Do not text, tweet, let it vibrate, anything at all. Turn it off. The light from the phone is very annoying in a dark theatre. If someone else's phone is going off, make sure you stare at them.

4. Don't eat anything

Whatever show it is, you will get through without starving.

Cinema

Just like the theatre but you can eat. The actors can't hear you but the rest of the audience still can. Restrain yourself.

Museums and art galleries

All the usual rules plus:

1. Don't eat or drink

You could damage something.

2. Don't wear a rucksack

You could damage something.

3. Don't touch any of the exhibits

Unless it is clearly a 'hands-on' exhibition. If you are not sure then it isn't.

4. Would it kill you to take off your baseball cap?

OK, that is not a rule. I was only asking.

5. Try not to stand or walk in the way of others

It's nice if everyone can enjoy the exhibition.

6. Try to restrain your own loud critique of the work

You are not on show. Maybe save your brilliant opinions for a quiet moment with a friend who cares what you think.

7. Do take kids with you

Taking children to a museum is a marvellous idea. Taking children to a museum and not taking the time to engage them with the place is a terrible idea.

The beach or the park

1. Dress the part

Consider the people around you. There are very few nudist beaches in the UK and they are clearly marked. You will be in no doubt if you are on one. There are, as far as I know, no nudist parks.

You may also want to consider the consequences before challenging someone else to strip off. In 2004 a sociology professor at Mars Hill College in North Carolina was teaching a class about social norms. He explained that in '99 per cent of American culture, public nudity is unacceptable'. He went on to tell the students that none of them would dare take their clothes off in front of their classmates even if he offered them an A grade. One student disagreed, disrobed and the professor had to ask 'to activate his retirement'. The student did not get an A.

2. Let everyone enjoy the natural setting

Some people like the sound of seagulls or the rustling of leaves and may not enjoy your music selection. You are outdoors for a reason. It's full of wonderful natural sounds – waves, wind and whatnot. It would also be terrible if you needed to call for help and all anyone could hear was Bon Jovi's greatest hits. If you must have music try to think about your selection. Maybe some lyrics you enjoy won't be quite the thing for the small children playing nearby.

3. You are relaxing not trying to conquer the place

Consider the amount of space you take up. Some people like to cordon off great areas of beach with windbreaks. This is really unkind to others. It is equally offensive in a large wide open space to plonk yourself right next to someone else. Let everyone breathe and try not to get sand on other people's sandwiches.

4. Remember – children can be stupid, including your own children

If you are an adult and you bring a child to the beach or a park with a pond, you are responsible for them. You need to make sure that they:

- Don't annoy other people.

- Don't drown. This is the case even if there is a lifeguard. You need to know the swimming capability of any children in your care and make sure they stay within it.

5. Remember – dogs can be stupid, including your own dog

Same rules as kids really. Noise can be very annoying and do pick up any mess.

6. Don't feed the birds

They will deposit white guano on you and try to eat your picnic. They don't have enough manners to only eat what they are given. When you leave, the birds will still hang around and annoy others. They won't have spotted that it was only you who was interested in feeding them.

7. Clean up

It's lovely to have a picnic in a public place but you need to take any leftover scraps home with you. Leave nothing behind that wasn't there when you arrived. This includes the kids.

8. Sex on the beach

It's a nice cocktail. Let's leave it at that. Besides, sand can chafe.

Public swimming pool

A lot of beach etiquette can be transferred to the swimming pool, plus …

1. Have a rinse

See that sparkling water? Showering before you get in the water means you can help keep the pool clean.

2. Do be excused before getting in the pool

Why shouldn't you wee in the pool? Apart from being icky there is some science. Pools have chlorine in them to kill waterborne bacteria and viruses. Urine has nitrogen in it which destroys chlorine molecules. It's bad manners to cause strangers to get sick. Pooing is even worse. If a baby is not toilet-trained, put a nappy on it.

3. Don't lap dance

If someone is trying to swim laps in a nice straight line, don't get in the way. There are usually separate lanes for this and you shouldn't be in them if you don't want to swim lengths.

4. Do be thoughtful

It's not just kids who can splash too much. Grown-ups swimming enthusiastically can do it as well.

5. Learn how to swim properly

No one should have to risk their life saving you because you didn't pay attention during lessons. The legendary funny man W. C. Fields started his career as what was known as a 'huckster' comedian. According to biographer Wes D. Gehring, when W. C. was fourteen he got a job at Fortescue's Pier in Atlantic City as a juggler and part-time drowner. When the pier was crowded Fields juggled for ten dollars a week. When attendance was low he would wade out into the water, pretend to drown and wait to be rescued. A crowd would gather to watch the excitement and the management would sell beer and food to the excited throng. Some days Fields drowned three or four times. This is no longer considered a reasonable occupation.

The sports field

1. Wear clean kit

Sweat from a previous engagement does not improve with age.

2. Don't fight

Either with other players or the ref.

3. Don't spit

Really – how much phlegm can you have that you need to gob on the pitch?

4. Help an opponent who is injured

Be nice. It's only a game.

5. Be a good sport

Over-celebrating makes you look as though you're surprised to have been good at something. Celebrating an opponent's error is just bad form. They feel bad enough. If you lose or are out then depart the field of play gracefully. Also admit when you've made a mistake. Be gracious. Shake hands.

6. Consider reading a book

I have to put my hand up and say I'm not very keen on sport. You may have gathered this from the suggestions above. I wish we had all descended from the species *Australopithecus sediba*, an early human ancestor thought to be too pigeon-toed to run. Good manners prevent me from mentioning this at sporting events.

Heavens, we've been busy. I expect that about now, everyone is thinking about

BEING EXCUSED

The average adult produces 1.5 litres of urine every twenty-four hours. Usually the urge to relieve oneself of this liquid is after the bladder has accumulated about 200 ml. It is not uncommon for people to need to be excused somewhere between four and seven times a day. This means that it is unlikely for everyone to be able to 'do their business', as my grandmother used to say, in the privacy of their own home.

Just because going to the toilet is something everyone does doesn't mean it's an occupation everyone wants to know about.

Rules for boys/men

1. Don't wee in the street

2. Ever

Everything about it is unpleasant – the smell, the sight, the residue. Would you be shocked if a woman suddenly squatted in the street and relieved herself? (Yes. Remember the fascination for even the non-sports fan when Paula Radcliffe took a 'bathroom break' in the street during the 2005 London Marathon?) However thrilled you may be with it, gentlemen, no one wants to see your penis in public.

3. Go for *Apis*

Considering men and boys have a built-in system for aiming their urine into a receptacle, it is amazing how often they miss. It used to be (and may still be for all I know) common for manufacturers to paint a bumblebee at the best spot for a man's aim on a urinal. It was a joke. The Latin for bumblebee is *Apis*.

Public lavatories

When you get to my age life seems little more than one long march to and from the lavatory.

Arthur Christopher Benson (1862–1925), English writer

Public lavatories are a good idea. They've been a good idea since Roman times when the Roman emperor Vespasian (ruled 69–79 AD) imposed a tax on the urine sold from public urinals in Rome's *Cloaca Maxima* (great sewer) system. There were plenty of people who wanted to buy the stuff. Urine contains ammonia and it was used by washer women to keep togas white. People have been 'spending a penny' in Britain since the Great Exhibition of 1851, when engineer George Jennings installed the first public toilets at Crystal Palace. They were known as 'Monkey Closets' and for a penny a visitor could get a clean seat, a towel, a comb and a shoe shine.

Public loos stop people weeing in the street, but there are a few guidelines about their use.

1. Give a little space

If there are lots of cubicles available don't choose the one right next to one that is already occupied. It makes people feel awkward.

2. Don't chat

If you enter a public loo with someone it is OK to stop your conversation until you reach the hand-washing stage. Some people prefer to get on with their weeing, etc., without chatter.

A bathroom break

My favourite public loo story (oddly enough I have several) concerns the eccentric American actress Tallulah Bankhead (who died in 1968). She was in a cubicle in a public loo with no paper, so she asked the woman next door if she had any. The woman said she didn't. Tallulah then asked if she had any tissues. No, the woman did not. Finally Tallulah enquired, 'My dear, have you two fives for a ten?'

3. Don't wee on the seat

It's a seat. It is not the depositing area. If you make a splash, wipe it down. If you leave a mess in the bowl, clean it where possible.

4. Dispose of the disposable

If you have to throw something away such as a tampon then wrap it neatly in paper and put it in the correct receptacle. Every public loo will have one.

5. Flush

If the loo is automatic, check that it has flushed.

6. Paper alert

Warn someone if there is no paper, but discreetly.

7. Don't hog the mirror in front of the basin

Someone may want to wash their hands. They may also not want your hair in the basin.

There are so many other public places where you might need to share space with others. Sadly I can't go through them all. There are probably quite specific rules about casinos and karaoke bars which I am unfamiliar with. This then, is a really good time to recall the Top Cs of life:

Consideration
Common sense
Context
Comfort

In 1624 the poet John Donne reminded the world that

No man is an island, entire of itself; every man is a piece of the continent, a part of the main.

If you don't want to live alone, make sure other people don't wish you did. Being part of humanity is a splendid business if you do it right. Hopefully you will be ready by the time you grow up, so let's take a look at what happens when you first leave home.

Much love

Sandi

6: TRAVEL

There are no foreign lands. It is the traveller only who is foreign.

Robert Louis Stevenson, *The Silverado Squatters* (1883)

Dear Mary

For many young people, certainly many middle-class young people, the first travel you will do without your parents takes place during the 'gap year'. The same basic rules that will apply when you're older apply now too. Those of us waiting at home won't expect you to be in constant contact. Instead, we might think about you by, for example, being nice to visitors in our own country: helping with directions, being charming and hoping this is happening to you and any other loved ones somewhere else in the world. (I have no idea if karma really works but I am hedging my bets.)

THE GAP YEAR

The gap year is not really a modern invention. There was something very similar which came into fashion in about 1660 and for the next couple of hundred years the Grand Tour of Europe was seen as an educational rite of passage for upper-class young men before they went off to learn upper-class things at

Oxbridge. Nowadays a gap year involves travelling to destinations that are much more far-flung.

Broadening the mind

The world is a book and those who do not travel read only one page.

St Augustine

There is nothing more annoying to the narrow-minded bigot than travelling. As soon as you head away from everything that is familiar, as soon as you widen your horizons, you begin to see that there are many ways to live a life and that they all have different things to commend them. The bigot hates this and so tends to stay in a tight little area of familiarity. I think, however, that it is the height of bad manners to presume that what you eat, what you think and what you believe, are the only ways to conduct yourself upon this glorious planet. If you wish to avoid such appalling bad behaviour you need to go exploring. Go in search of places beyond your ken and if you open your eyes and ears you will return a much nicer and more interesting person.

P.S. It doesn't have to be expensive. If you really have no money, take the bus from the end of your road and go somewhere you hadn't thought of before. If you have less than no money walk in a direction that is not a usual route. I would happily spend a year just exploring the Mile End Road in London. It has been a thoroughfare for hundreds of years and is packed with interesting sights. So, no excuses …

Get on with it and go

The killing of time is the worst of murders.

Daniel Defoe

Considering how precious life is, it is astonishing how much time humans waste. A recent review of how long players have been occupied by the video game 'Angry Birds' discovered that if you added together all the time spent on it worldwide, then fans of the game had played it for 200,000 years. Don't keep wishing you could go somewhere. Go!

The other

The first thing that may happen as you step outside your possibly small circle of experience is that you will encounter the unfamiliar. If there is one thing more inclined to cause conflict than anything else, it is when someone comes up against something, as the Americans say, that is 'outside their comfort zone'. In general I think of it as 'The Other'. It includes other ways of thinking, other ways of worshipping and other ways of setting one's moral compass. The worst thing that can happen to people confronted with 'the other' is that they begin to fear the thing they do not know. This fear can lead to a position of disagreement based on nothing more than ignorance. Stay in that ignorant state long enough and blind prejudice will soon pop along. Once it settles in, blind prejudice doesn't need a lot of help to step up to conflict.

Having respect for difference seems to me one of the ultimate goals of having good manners. I find myself amazed at those who believe that they alone are right, that they alone are the person to whom some higher power has decided to tell the truth. Make no mistake, I have very clear views, but I am more than happy to be challenged about them.

The unfamiliar is no excuse for bad manners. People who are different from ourselves have the same right to respect as we do. We all differ in so many ways – gender, race, culture, religion, sexual orientation, intelligence, height, eye colour, hair colour, fashion sense, strength, whether we like lentils or not (you and I, Mary, both loathe them): no two people are exactly the same. Yet instead of embracing such diversity, society develops ...

Prejudice

The very ink with which history is written is merely fluid prejudice.

Mark Twain (1835–1910), American author

I know I seem a bit keen on the origin of words, but I think etymology tells you something about the sense behind the way in which we express ourselves. Prejudice comes from the Medieval Latin (*mea culpa*) *prejudicium* which means 'injustice'. Being prejudiced suggests you have made up your mind before you have the facts and that you have been unfair in the process.

It's an odd thing, prejudice. It happens all the time, but if you take the long view of history you'll find that a society which has taken a blinkered attitude does often eventually realise that they made a mistake. I don't think anyone needs to be reminded about what happened to the Jewish population of Europe during the Second World War and how hard the German nation has worked towards a more tolerant future. I know I was not alone in my delight that America overcame its appalling record on the rights of its black citizens to elect Barack Obama.

Prejudice is small-mindedness personified. History teaches us that we should not be afraid of the other and yet the fear lives on. Many find change of any kind unsettling, but as someone once said, change is inevitable except from a vending machine. Try your best:

1. Not to be sanctimonious

If you have a strong belief, don't condemn those who don't. There are approximately 1.1 billion people on earth who do not have a religious belief. Their lack of belief deserves the same respect as your faith. We are all entitled to decide for ourselves. It is just possible that you may die and find you were wrong. So far no one has come back from the dead with definitive proof of anything.

2. Not to knock someone else's beliefs

There are twenty-one major religions in the world. Don't be judgemental about someone else's fundamental beliefs. Try to listen instead. Knowing the historical background to anyone's beliefs is always helpful.

3. To guard against xenophobia

Xenophobia is a fear of foreigners. It's a dislike of anything seen as foreign or strange. It is often irrational. Xenophobes become afraid that foreigners will overwhelm them, cause them to lose their own identity or somehow infringe on their own lives. They won't. Be careful you are not being racist. No one is superior to another human being simply because of their particular skin pigment.

When dealing with something or someone 'other'

- Don't stare.
- Don't stereotype.
- Don't ask questions you wouldn't like to be asked yourself.
- Don't be mean.
- Don't assume superiority.

All of the above can be summarised into two words – Have Respect.

Now let's get out there.

GETTING PLACES

Summer and winter, travel in cars and boats is an excellent test of politeness, patience and inborn refinement and delicacy. It has been often remarked that there would not be nearly as many unhappy marriages in the United States, if lovers would journey together before the all-important vows are made.

'Daisy Eyebright', *A Manual of Etiquette with Hints on Politeness and Good Breeding* (Sophia Orne Johnson, 1826–99)

AEROPLANES

Heavier-than-air flying machines are impossible.

Lord Kelvin, President, Royal Society, 1895.

The first woman passenger to ascend into the air was Élisabeth Thible who, on 4 June 1784, took off in a hot-air balloon in Lyon, France. Élisabeth was an opera singer and she and the balloonist, Monsieur Fleurant, were marking a visit to the town by King Gustav III of Sweden. She was dressed for the occasion as the Roman goddess Minerva and as they ascended, Élisabeth sang two arias while continuing to fuel the balloon's fire box.

Air travel has since lost a lot of its glamour. I travelled a lot on planes as a child, making my first trip from Europe to Africa when I was just six weeks old. Back in the 1960s and 1970s, air travel was still seen as rather glamorous. Passengers dressed up for the occasion. Today a lot of flights resemble the worst kind of coach travel with people turning into herded animals as they scramble for seats. This descent into travel hell doesn't mean we should simply abandon all attempts at civil behaviour at check-in. There are still a few niceties which will help overcome some of the horrors:

Boarding

1. Your bag

There was a time when nice men in peaked caps took care of your luggage. Now you must be your own porter and in many instances take your bag into the cabin with you. There is a size limit. There is a size limit for a reason. Oddly enough the cabin also has a limited size. Don't take up more room than you are entitled to. Pack light.

2. Be ready

Don't keep everyone waiting because you can't find your travel documents.

3. Mind the aisle

Aeroplane aisles are narrow places. Carry your bag in front of you so that you can make sure not to hit anyone with it. You may have to sit next to them for the next ten hours and they may seek revenge.

4. Stick to your space

Don't fill someone else's overhead locker space just because they haven't boarded yet. How would you feel if someone did that to you? If you have to move someone's things, ask them first. Just because they have no manners doesn't mean you need to fall at this particular hurdle.

5. Settle in quickly

Everyone has luggage to stow and seat belts to put on and there is an actual departure time which is helpfully printed on your ticket. A great way to speed things up is to have a small plastic bag prepared with everything you need in-flight – glasses, book, medication – which you can quickly slip into the seat pocket in front of you.

6. Turn off your electronic equipment

All you need to know is that it may or may not do something funny to the plane's controls. For all I know the pilot just wants to concentrate and not have several hundred passengers shouting 'I'm on a plane!' down their mobiles while he's dealing with air traffic control. Who cares what it is? One of the few pleasures left in airline travel is that it is a zone where no one can use their mobile to ring anyone (although 'Airplane mode' does still allow for other forms of irritating behaviour at 40,000 feet).

In flight

1. More stuff about space

Planes are cramped places. It's like sitting at table except that you have been allocated a small, sometimes really small, space in a long metal tube. Armrests are for sharing; your music is not.

2. Very small table manners

All the usual rules apply – you know, proper cutlery use, napkin, no gnashing of teeth, etc. – plus you need to be careful that those ridiculous containers in which airline food comes don't splash or erupt on your neighbour. If they do, apologise and offer to pay for any dry-cleaning.

3. Odour

It's nice to be clean when you share a public space. Consider your feet. Many people take their shoes off in-flight. If you are a person given to foot odour (and there is no way you won't be sure) bring some kind of sock to wear while your shoes are off.

4. The person beside you

Be polite, but don't start telling some poor stranger beside you your life story. Let them have at least a hint of privacy. Don't try to read the screen on their laptop or a page of their book. Don't spread your paperwork out so much that they have no choice but to learn too much about you. Don't choose a window seat if your bladder is not a sturdy friend to you. No one wants to keep getting up and down to let you use the facilities. If someone is boring you, politely tell them that you need to rest, work or something else distracting.

5. The person behind you

Imagine how far you would like the seat in front to recline if you still want to be comfortable. Use that as a guide for your own seat.

6. The person in front

Don't kick them or grab the back of their seat in order to stand up. Use the armrest.

7. The aisle

Don't block it by standing chatting to other people. If the crew are trying to get past with refreshments, many people may hate you if you come between them and a drink.

8. Don't get drunk

I never know why some airlines make such a big deal about their wine list in First and Business class. At altitude almost everything tastes exactly the same. The only real difference is that you get drunk more quickly.

9. Don't have sex in front of the other passengers

Suddenly you realise why we need rules at all. Isn't it amazing that I even have to write such a statement? Sadly, some people need reminding and you won't be surprised to learn that this rather led on from no. 8.

In October 1999, greeting cards executive David Machin and computer company exec Amanda Holt were arrested in Manchester after disembarking from an American Airlines flight from Dallas. They had performed 'sex acts' on each other and refused to stop even when requested by the crew. According to the stewardess's report, one passenger, a woman of sixty-five making her first flight, wanted to know if such activity was commonplace. Both David and Amanda eventually lost their jobs. Hard to think what greeting card David's friends might have sent him after that. Some commentators thought that the worst part was that it took place in Business class.

10. The happy room

On one particularly enjoyable sojourn in Thailand my host instructed me to refer to the toilet as 'The Happy Room'. He said it was the one place guaranteed to make people more cheerful after they had been there. Plane 'Happy Rooms' are tiny and not suitable for a makeover of your hair, your clothing or your face. Sort out the essentials and go and sit down again. Sadly, they are usually too small to provide a useful way round rule no. 9.

Deplaning

Deplaning is one of my least favourite words. I know that it means 'getting off the plane' but somehow it suggests some wizard carpentry move.

A sobering story

In 2010 a small plane carrying twenty-one people was en route from Kinshasa to Bandundu in the Democratic Republic of the Congo. One of the passengers had packed more hand luggage than is normally considered sensible. He had put a crocodile in a duffle bag which then escaped during the flight. Not surprisingly, the terrified passengers tried to get away from the unexpected guest, they rushed to the front of the plane which then sadly crashed. Only one person survived along with the crocodile. He then lost his life to a machete. (The croc, not the surviving passenger.)

1. Opening the bins

Calling the overhead lockers 'bins' is also unpleasant but whatever you call them, they do need some thought. The crew will tell you that some items may have shifted in the bins during a flight and you should be careful. They don't just tell you this to annoy you.

Be careful. See if anyone else (a short person, like myself) needs any help. Don't take someone else's luggage. Nothing they have is likely to fit you.

2. Wait your turn

Everyone wants to get off. Hardly anyone ever wishes they could linger on a plane.

3. Be ready

Sure as eggs is eggs you need your travel documents at least twice on a flight – at the beginning and at the end. Don't act as though it is a surprise.

MANNERS ABROAD

Don't

1. Be a tosser

Don't go on a huge night out and be completely rowdy, inappropriate and thuggish in a new place. Have a nice night but don't go overboard. It gives Brits abroad a bad name.

2. Think it will be just like home

Don't get angry if you lose mobile phone reception. There are, thank heavens, still remote parts of the world where you won't be able to text, call or tweet. Deal with it. Enjoy it. It might do you good. You may also not be able to get your favourite food or drink. Remember why you came travelling in the first place. It wasn't so that you could just live the same life as you do at home. One of the greatest days to experience anywhere in the world is New Year in Bali. It's called *Nyepi* and the entire country falls silent for a day. Wonderful.

Do

1. Research the place that you are visiting

Learn customs, rituals and faux pas that may cause offence in your new surroundings. Make an effort, then if you make a mistake people will be quick to forgive you. Apart from that, you will get so much more out of your visit.

2. Consider the single traveller

If you are travelling with someone or in a group and you see a single traveller – invite them out with you if you are going for dinner or drinks. Travelling by yourself can be hard and takes a lot of courage. An invitation makes the person far from home feel welcome and not so lonely. They might be delightful. You might have masses in common.

Sussing the shibboleth

A car is useless in New York, essential everywhere else. The same with good manners.

Mignon McLaughlin (1913–83), American author

There is probably a survey about almost everything. There are no doubt surveys about surveys. Anyway, I once read a report about a survey concerning how often travellers in various cities around the world said 'please' and 'thank you' while buying tickets. In London it was 70 per cent, Tokyo 50 per cent, Hamburg 30 per cent and in New York just 10 per cent. It's probably nonsense, but based on this information you might think a couple of things:

- People in New York have no manners.

- People in London have too much time on their hands.

Neither is entirely true. To be honest I think more Londoners say 'cheers' than 'thank you' and I have come across plenty of New York charm. All modes of behaviour have to be put in some kind of cultural context (there's one of your Top Cs again) and you need to be sensitive if you want to work out what it is. Every culture will have some custom or practice that will betray you as an outsider. It's called:

Shibboleth

This is more of an idea than a word. It's about the tiny nuances that separate one culture from another. Human beings at their core are all much the same, but we vary in small degrees – what we wear, what we like to eat, exactly what we think is rude or polite. These tiny details are not always immediately apparent, and spending time working out what they are is part of the fun of travel. Knowing that the devil is in the detail may stop you stepping all over a way of life you're not familiar with.

The concept of 'shibboleth' has ancient roots. Somewhere around 1370–1070 BC (so long ago people were counting backwards) there was a fight between the Israelites of Gilead and the Israelites of Ephraim. It would have been nice if they could have got along as they had that Israelite thing in common, but there we are. There was a battle and the Gileadites won. The Ephraimites decided it was best to head back over the River Jordan from where they had come. Now the two tribes spoke similar languages but had very different accents. One of the main differences was that the Ephraimites couldn't pronounce the sound sh. The Hebrew word *shibbólet* just means the part of a plant which contains grains. So an ear of corn is a shibboleth. The Gileadites and Ephraimites looked rather alike, so in order to distinguish who was the enemy, each time a Gileadite soldier caught someone trying to escape he asked him to say the word shibbólet. If he couldn't, he was clearly an Ephraimite. According to the Book of Judges 'forty-two thousand Ephraimites fell on this occasion'.

Hopefully, we don't kill anyone these days just over a little pronunciation issue, but understanding about shibboleth is still a good idea. On the whole you will be just fine if you make it clear that you are interested in another person's way of life and doing your best to be both friendly and respectful. You are a guest in someone else's country. If you can't cope with anything you are not used to, then it's a good job you're trying to expand your mind by travelling.

Just remember that no one, not even a foreigner, really likes rude behaviour. Consider the village of Lheraule in northern France. In 2012, the mayor, Gerard Plee, concerned about politeness, introduced new regulations which allowed for citizens to be ejected from the town hall if they didn't say 'hello' or 'thank you'. He said the rules were aimed at 'the eternally dissatisfied, the rancorous and any other grumpy people'.

Learning the language

Try to grasp at least a few basics – Please, Thank you, Sorry, Excuse me, How are you? Are you married? etc. Everyone appreciates the effort and there are wonderful words which are unique to each culture; words which tell you something about the people whose home you are visiting. It's also worth checking that you aren't making an embarrassing mistake.

Rachel Millet was the most marvellous woman and if you have time, do read about her. She drove a mobile hospital during the Second World War and eventually married a French officer call René Millet in 1946. He joined the French diplomatic service and together they had many foreign postings. In Bangkok her poor grasp of Thai rather famously caused her to mispronounce the word for bread rolls so that her VIP guests sat down to a soup garnished with ping-pong balls.

Check local customs. Be ready to swallow the shibboleth.

DINING ABROAD

Committing santi

As we have so many rules about eating, there are endless stories about food and drink being served abroad in a novel manner which the narrow-minded traveller is appalled by. In her book on modern manners written in 1872, Eliza Cheadle tells a rather shocking story about an English woman visiting the French author Madame Du Bocage in Paris in the eighteenth century. Madame attempted to serve tea *à l'anglaise* to her guest and when the 'spout of the teapot did not pour freely; she bade the footman blow into it!' You can almost feel Eliza shuddering.

Sharing food with someone from a totally different background is a great privilege and you need to let go of some preconceived notions about what is or isn't acceptable. If you don't, no one will have a good time. Take the Hausa people, who are one of the largest ethnic groups scattered across West Africa. The men wear fabulous embroidered gowns called *babban riga*. They are Muslim, so no pork will ever be served. Food can be scarce and this means it needs to be treated with respect. Making a trivial remark such as complimenting someone on their clothing during a meal is known as committing 'santi'. To the Hausa it makes the diner look ridiculous. Whilst eating with the Hausa you need to pay attention to the food.

Eating with your hands

In other parts of the world eating with the fingers has never disappeared. The best guess one can make is that about a third of the world's population don't use cutlery, but there are always rules to keep things clean. I once had a very pleasant meal in a room above a garage in Ghana. The food was served in a communal washing up bowl and we were expected to eat from it with our hands. First, however, an identical plastic bowl containing water was passed around so that everyone could clean their dusty fingers.

Check the local customs. Be aware, for example, that in parts of India, Africa and the Middle East you should only touch the plate with your right hand. Wherever you are, don't finger the food other people are going to eat. However clean you think your mitts are, other people may not be so sure.

Alcohol

Almost all cultures view imbibing alcohol alone with suspicion. The Lele of Zaire disapprove of drunkenness because it shows you didn't share. Drinking booze is generally seen as a communal activity. It is meant to be friendly, which is why there are so many forms of greeting when consuming alcohol – *Santé, Slainte, Salud, C'in C'in, Prost, Skol, Salute, L'chaim, Cheers* and so on. The ancient Egyptians drank together from a communal pot using long straws. In the UK drinks in pubs are bought in 'rounds'. There is a similar system in many societies. The Greeks call it *kerasmata* while the French refer to *la tournée*. Everyone must take their turn to buy, which not only shares the costs but helps organise the amount everyone in a group is drinking.

Turning down food offerings

I have eaten all manner of things I didn't like the look of. So far nothing has killed me and in general it was an interesting experience. I don't recommend locusts or bull's testicles but I'm glad I had a go. Don't turn things down just because you've never tried them before. If you really think you can't manage it, tell a small white lie – 'I've just eaten', 'I'm vegetarian', something that won't offend. If you think something is unhygienic make sure you are not having a knee-jerk reaction. I spent a month travelling in the Sudan. On most street corners there would be a woman making coffee on a small open fire. Often her cooking pot was fashioned from an old coffee tin and the drink was served in small shot glasses. None of the film crew I travelled with would touch the stuff, but our local driver advised me to ask the women for 'coffee with medicine' – a strong coffee mixed with a large teaspoon of ginger. I had one every morning and I was the only person on the trip who didn't get sick. It was a pleasure each morning to squat beside a fire and wait for my drink. To this day I put ginger in my morning coffee.

Foreigners can be funny

I was once filming in the Arctic for the BBC. We were out with a party hunting ptarmigan, a large bird which doesn't take much hunting. A poor fowl was duly dispatched and the hunter set about preparing the bird for us to eat. He removed the small, whole heart and placed it in a glass of vodka. 'Here,' he said, handing me the glass, 'it is good luck to eat the heart while it is still warm.' I could think of nothing more revolting, but not wishing to offend I put the piece of offal in my mouth and swallowed with a gulp. The locals all watched silently and then cried with laughter because I had believed them.

Tipping

Make sure it's the custom. It may seem like a nice gesture but in some countries, such as Japan and Korea, it is actually considered insulting.

PERSONAL SPACE

It's worth noting that the 'circles of attention' in which we all live vary in size in different cultures. In some countries it is common to stand very close to one another while in others such proximity would be considered rude. Observe the people around you and try to adjust your own circle accordingly. You may also need to be tolerant of those from other cultures who come closer than you are used to. They're unlikely to bite.

Hand gestures

I've already explained that making your thumb and forefinger into a circle – either to remember which bit of bread is yours at a dinner table or to signal OK – can be an insult in most of South America and suggests to a Turk that he is homosexual. Check your gestures. The V-sign in the UK has the same meaning as raising the middle finger in the US, and the Greeks find gesturing with an open palm offensive. If in doubt, keep your hands in your pocket and smile. OK?

Handshakes

This can be a bit of minefield so check out the local customs. Some countries, such as the Philippines, regard a hearty handshake as an aggressive gesture. Some religions have handshaking rules:

* **Orthodox Jews** won't shake hands with someone of the opposite sex.

* **A strict Muslim woman** will not shake hands with a man but

* **A strict Muslim man** will not shake hands with a non-Muslim woman.

Business cards

The business card is an important matter in many Asian countries. It is almost an extension of the person whose name it bears. Don't diss the card. Don't fold it, scribble on it, shove it in your pocket or use it to pick your teeth.

Shoes and feet

You might at first think it odd that after the first Gulf War a mosaic of President George Bush Snr was laid on the floor of the Al-Rashid Hotel in Baghdad. It wasn't, however, a tribute. Anyone who entered the hotel had to walk over his face and it was hard for the Iraqis to conceive a greater insult. In most of the Middle and Far East, it is considered an insult to point your feet (particularly the soles) at another person. Shoes are seen as dirty and the feet represent the lowest part of the body. During Colonel Gaddafi of Libya's first interview with Tony Blair in March 2007, Gaddafi insulted the British prime minister by crossing his legs so that the sole of his shoe was facing his guest. When Saddam Hussein fell from power many of the celebrations involved Iraqi people beating statues of their former leader with their shoes.

There are many places such as Japan and parts of the Middle East where you must take off your shoes at the door. This is also the case in some Scandinavian houses, particularly in the winter when you might track snow and slush into the house. A clue is often the pile of shoes at the door.

GIVING GIFTS

The word 'gift' is yet another example of the Nordic people leaving their mark on the English. It comes from Old Norse and can mean either gift or good luck. I like the association with good luck as giving a gift is often a very successful way of helping to make new friendships and to cement old ones. There are some countries where the correct giving of gifts could fill an entire book and, frankly, I lack the time. The Japanese, for example,

consider gift-giving a vital part of showing respect and apprecia-
tion. All you need to know is that it is very important. If you are in
any doubt, check in advance. As a visitor you're likely to be given
some leeway. I always take tins of English tea. Even if they don't
like the tea, the tin is nice.

That's enough of the theory. Now you need to go and explore
for yourself. The world is an astonishing place full of sights you
cannot imagine. There is not a photograph in the world that can
capture what it feels like to stand on the rim of the Grand Canyon,
there is not a single restaurant in Europe which can replicate the
taste sensation of freshly caught prawns sizzled in sweet basil and
served on a Thai beach, and you will never look at light again in
the same way until you have headed north in search of an Arctic
sky. Go explore. But please, don't forget to write.

Much love

Sandi

7: SHOULDER TO THE GRINDSTONE

Dear Mary

I have extolled the virtues of travel and exploring the world but failed to mention one critical point – someone has to pay for it. One of the many irksome things about being a grown-up is that you are likely to have to work for a living. If you are not independently wealthy then you must do two things – blame your parents and go to seek employment. Adults will tell you that there is a high chance that the harder you work the more money you will have. Sadly it is true. It may also be that you need to prepare for this world of work with a period of further education, so we may need to get you ready for …

BEING A STUDENT

I have never let my schooling interfere with my education.

Mark Twain (1835–1910)

Going into higher education is a wonderful opportunity to expand your mind and learn to take responsibility for you own life. Lots of the guidelines you have already mastered apply but there are a few extras to help you make a success of your academic years. It should be a wonderful time. It is unlikely that you will have the experience that the Iraqi-American Ibrahim al-Marashi did when a graduate student. He wrote an article entitled *Iraq's Security & Intelligence Network: A Guide & Analysis* which was published in 2002. I suspect he had no idea that this piece of work would be plagiarised and used by the British government to justify invading Iraq a year later. I doubt your student days will have quite that impact but be careful just in case.

1. Don't fall asleep in lectures

No matter how hung-over you are. Your lecturer is not a robot. It's nice to show a little respect.

2. Don't hog the computers in the library facility

The computers are to be shared. They are there to help you get an education, not update your Facebook page or play solitaire. Don't lock the computer while you go off and have a three-hour lunch break so that no one else can get access.

3. Don't keep a library book past its return date

Libraries exist for the sharing of books. Someone else may want to read it.

4. Do the work you've been set

There is no point in being at university if you don't want to study. It's very irritating to everyone else if you've failed to pay attention and keep asking silly questions because you can't catch up.

5. Don't be mean

It's unusual for someone at university to have a lot of money. If someone buys a round of drinks, make sure you return the favour.

THE WORKPLACE

Hi ho hi ho, it's off to work we go.

Sneezy, Sleepy, Dopey, Doc, Happy, Bashful & Grumpy
Snow White and the Seven Dwarfs, 1937

I hope you will have a chance to go to a place of further education where you can expand your mind and make friends who will last a lifetime. It's not, however, for everyone. Some people can't afford it while others simply want to get on into the workplace as soon as possible. Whether you are a graduate or not you will probably need to seek employment rather than having some well-paid gig land at your feet. Who knows what that gig will be. Ideally it will be something that is both stimulating and profitable. Life is too short to be bored so I wish you a career that you enjoy. I doubt you'll get a job underground with cartoon characters but wouldn't it be fun? Whatever work you aim for, in order to get it you may have to face a ...

Job interview

It is not possible to overestimate how important good manners can be when you are looking for work. The competition for most jobs is now very fierce indeed. The employer has the upper hand as they scan the CVs of applicants who are often overqualified for even the most menial of tasks. The chances are they will select the person who seems the most amenable. So bearing in mind the stiff opposition you need to ...

1. Have a good CV
Make sure your CV is neatly laid out and printed nicely. Check your spelling and your grammar. That bit of paper could change your life.

2. Be on time
No one is going to employ you if you can't even get to an interview on time. Bad traffic or transport problems are not a

good enough excuse. Allow extra time for things to go wrong. If you are early then you will have plenty of time to get yourself into a calm frame of mind for the interview.

3. Look good

Dress appropriately for the workplace. Make an effort. No one wants to work with someone who can't be bothered. If the interview takes place over a meal try to stay looking good. Don't order pasta with a heavy sauce or anything else which might land on your best clothes. Remember all your table manners and what a bad influence alcohol can be.

4. Pay attention

The rules are the same as those for any kind of important encounter – turn your phone off, sit up, smile, listen and respond. If you find that hard, think about how many other people are going to be sitting in the same place trying to get the job instead of you.

5. Be friendly but not familiar

The person interviewing you may end up as your boss. They are not best friend material. Be pleasant but respectful.

6. Be positive

Let the interviewer know your good qualities. Don't be shy about why you would be the best person for the job.

Behaving at work

It's hard to know when human beings first had a sense of 'going to work'. Did a caveman wake up on a Monday morning wishing he could be a hunter instead of a cave painter? Certainly the concept of work is not a new one. It's actually holidays that are a relatively modern notion. I had a Danish great-aunt who was a milkmaid in Jutland. When she got married she and her husband had a week in Copenhagen. No one from the very rural area she came from had ever been to the capital city but when she returned no one asked what it was like. They wanted to know what it was like to have a week off.

About 38 million people work in the UK and it would be great if they behaved themselves. There are many places of work – shops, offices, theatres, restaurants, garages, factories, etc. and the same general thoughts about behaviour apply in most instances.

1. Dress appropriately

It's good to be yourself, but sometimes making a big statement can get in the way. My father was a very famous broadcaster on Danish television. In the 1970s he grew a beard and he received several letters complimenting him on his new hirsute look. He immediately shaved his face. When I asked him why he replied, 'I'm a journalist. If people are looking at my beard then they're not listening to what I am saying.'

2. Respect other people's time

It's just the same as when you go for an interview. Every time you are late you are wasting someone else's life. Be punctual. Turn up on time for work so that everyone can get on. If you make an appointment, arrive on time or even a bit early. If you're going to be late, always call and let them know. Try not to miss deadlines. If you keep missing them, then sit down with your boss and work out what the problem is. Who was it who said one should under-promise and over-deliver? Probably someone who got promoted.

3. Don't be grumpy

If you arrive at work every day saying you wish you weren't there then it won't take long for everyone to wish it too. Park your attitude outside the door. If someone else is grumpy, try for a brief moment to imagine that they have a life outside the thrill of corporate life, about which you probably know nothing.

4. Don't abuse your position

If you are someone's boss that doesn't mean you can treat them badly. They are not your serf and you are not lord of your domain. You will get more out of someone if you treat them with respect. No one has to collect your dry-cleaning except you.

5. Have a think

The car-tyre calendar with naked women on is not appropriate even in a car-tyre place – and be very careful about jokes. It's that whole gender, race, sexuality issue. Hilarious to you maybe, but hurtful to someone else. Explain to the 'joker' why you find it hurtful. As for the joker – get back to work.

6. Be pleasant

Please, thank you, etc., for everyone from the lowliest employee to the boss. You could end up in either position. Why not congratulate those who've done well? Make sure those who deserve credit get it. What's the harm? And if you are making yourself a hot drink it won't hurt you to put the kettle on for others. Hopefully they will return the favour.

The office

The word comes from ... (drum roll) ... Latin, of course. The word is *officium* but it doesn't really mean a place. It's a duty or obligation, a service of some kind. It's more the sort of office that comes to you. The first offices in history belonged to scribes. When writing was invented it was thought rather clever. These days anyone can blog away, but back then scribes and their magical way with words were kept in separate rooms. The office boom really took off in the industrial revolution. All those belching factories making goods led to loads more paperwork and more people started working in offices. Then someone invented the lift and soon you had multi-storied offices.

About 1 in 4 of the UK workforce now work in an office. If you work 40 hours a week for 48 weeks of the year then you will spend 1,920 hours at the office. Wow. Probably best not to think of that figure when you're going back to work on 2 January. That is a lot of time to spend with other people so ...

1. Get on with your job

Spending the first half an hour telling everyone about your night before is going to become tiresome. Wait till lunch before boring everyone with your private life so that they can get on with what they're paid to do. If you want to do well at your job then it's a good idea to do some actual work. Spending time on social networking sites is not going to be helpful and someone is bound to find out.

2. Try not to be annoying

If you have any bad habits such as drumming on the desk with your pen, try not to. Repetitive noises made by children are very irritating. Made by adults they are inexplicable. Don't tap, whistle, hum or anything else that will get on your colleagues' nerves. It can help break down barriers if you give your colleagues permission to tell you to shut up. Also on the annoying front – consider how many times you can ask your colleagues to 'sponsor' your charity walk/bike ride, etc. You may think that your walking the Great Wall of China will save the whale. Others may see it as a holiday paid for by sponsors.

3. Share stuff

For example, if you have a communal printer remember that everyone has to use it. Don't hog the whole printing queue and if the printer runs out of supplies, sort it.

4. Respect your colleagues' privacy

Sometimes people work in very crowded conditions – desks are very close together or booths back onto each other. It's hard for anyone to be private but give it a go – don't read other people's emails, don't check their post, don't listen in on their phone calls, don't borrow things from their desk without asking, don't eat their lunch. (Is that last one just me?) Keep your desk tidy and stick to your own area. If you can't then you will have to start your own business.

Being too nice to your co-workers

There was once an American sea captain called John Kendrick. He was quite a fellow. A bit of an explorer and reputed to have taken part in the Boston Tea Party which kick-started the American Revolution. By 1794 he had become a trader and in the December of that year he sailed his brig into Honolulu (then called Fair Haven). There were two British vessels there including the *Jackal* under Captain William Brown. Kendrick helped Brown sort out a local matter and the two men were grateful to each other. On 12 December Kendrick's brig fired a thirteen-gun salute. Brown replied in kind, shooting from the *Jackal*. Sadly, one of his cannons was loaded with real grapeshot and Kendrick was killed. OK, I get that this is an unlikely scenario in an office but try not to overdo things.

5. Keep it down

At the office, however important a phone call is to you, not everyone needs to hear about it. Have some volume control.

6. Don't eat at your desk

OK, this one can be difficult but really you will do a better day's work if you take an actual break. Eating *al desko* just means messing up your keyboard with crumbs and no one needs that patronising look from the exhausted IT guy. If you must eat, try to choose something inoffensive to other people's noses. Actually, beware smelling in general. If someone is causing hateful smells a quiet word may be best for everyone.

7. Don't shout

Don't yell a question across the office. If you need to speak to someone get up and go and talk to them. You don't need to involve everyone.

8. Don't talk behind someone's back in the office

They will find out and you will be sorry. If others are gossiping, do your best to walk away and not get involved.

9. Mind the tricky stuff

If you have to have a tricky conversation with someone then have it in private. Ideally warn the person in advance.

THE BUSINESS OF BUSINESS WRITING

I don't know to what extent one can believe the figures, but allegedly the average worker spends eighty-one days a year answering emails. That could be true, but then I have seen a survey that claims the average person spends three years of their life washing their underwear. Anyway, there is a lot of writing in modern business. The general rules about communication apply, with a few add-ons.

1. Don't ignore tricky emails

It's best just to reply quickly to emails and messages even if they are on the tricky side. Maybe draft a reply first. Be honest and polite.

2. Mind your temper

Don't email when you are cross. Don't do anything except punch a pillow. If you don't have a pillow in the office, get up from your desk and have a brief walk to calm yourself down.

3. Don't presume the person you are writing to is a man

The days should be behind us of writing 'Dear Sir' as a general greeting to a business contact you have never met.

4. Consider the time

In 2011, the car manufacturer Volkswagen decided to turn off staff email access half an hour after they left work and not turn it on again until half an hour before they started the next day. The French information technology services firm Atos have banned all internal emails as of 2014. You don't need to be available 24/7, you just need people to be clear about the timeframe within which you will respond. Don't email in the middle of the night – it encourages others to do the same. And it suggests you have no life.

5. Consider the recipient

Decide whether it would be better to talk to someone in person or whether an email is less interrupting. If you need to consider an email before replying, then write a quick reply saying when you will get back with a more considered response.

6. Emailing the wrong person

Bad idea in the first place. Apologise immediately. Try to repair the inevitable damage.

7. Be clear

Numbering your points in a business email helps to organise your viewpoint.

8. Be proper

Sign off nicely. A single 'cheers' at the end of an email can undo the simple act of a carefully considered communication.

WORKPLACE ROMANCE

This is usually not a good idea. If you are not the boss then you could find yourself out of a job if things go wrong. If you are the boss you could find yourself at the wrong end of a legal action. If you do fall in love at work it's quite straightforward:

* Keep it quiet and then

* One of you find somewhere else to work.

Everyone else has got a job to do and could do without you making doe eyes at someone.

But obviously if it does work out, yes they would like to come to the wedding, thanks.

Wherever you work it is good to follow the old adage of treating everyone as you would wish to be treated. This is certainly a good idea in confined spaces such as ...

The office party

Everyone who has ever worked in an office has a story about an office party gone wrong. The mistake many people make is thinking that this is a good time to relax. Here is the headline news on this:

You are still at a work event

If you don't want to destroy all the good work you have done throughout the year here are a few pointers:

1. Make an effort

This is a chance to look a little sharper than usual. Everyone may see you in a different and possibly better light.

2. Turn your phone off

It's a party.

3. Don't get drunk

(Can you spot a recurring theme yet?) If you want to make a good impression then getting legless is almost certainly not going to help. If you do plan to consume alcohol then eat a little something before you go, to line your stomach.

4. Connect

Use the opportunity to talk to people you don't know. They may be useful to you during a working day or even turn out to be good fun. There may be some shy co-workers who will be grateful if you chat with them. Make connections but remember, it's still a party. Don't talk shop or insurance or whatever it is you all do during 'office hours'.

5. Keep it light

It's a social occasion. Be social (see 'Conversation at the dinner table'), but don't be a creep by only talking to those in charge.

6. Don't make love

Actually don't even come on to anyone, least of all the boss or head of department. You will look an idiot and you will have to do a walk of shame in the morning. In fact every morning for some considerable time.

7. Beware social media

Think twice before appearing in a picture at the office party which someone is going to post on the internet. Don't post inappropriate pictures of others while you or they are drunk. Stay right away from the photocopier.

8. Say thank you

Nothing has changed since the time you went to your first kids' birthday party (see separate section). Someone invited you, someone organised it, someone needs to be thanked.

9. Saying goodbye

If the party is marking an employee's departure, try to be nice whatever you think of them. Writing 'This place won't be the same without you' in a leaving card is a good way of telling the truth whatever you think of someone. This is not the time to recall past irritations. They are leaving. It is fine.

The work function

The work function is about mingling, not profound conversations. It may be a cocktail party or a celebration of some kind but basically it is something you need to attend as part of your job. Often it takes the form of some kind of speed social event where people spend a short amount of time with someone else before moving on. It is about making connections and being seen to be seen. Try to remember you are not there for either the free food or to get drunk. Indeed it is about the worst place to get bladdered as everyone will talk about it for years afterwards. So …

1. Try to remember people's names

A simple trick is to look into their eyes and repeat their name out loud when you are told it. Theatrical people often call everyone 'Darling' because they can't remember the names of everyone they've worked with. Employ this technique with caution. If you work, for example, in a bus depot, it may come across as a little over the top.

2. Nurse your drink

We're really clear on the alcohol thing by now, aren't we?

3. Use the toothpicks provided

Canapés are often served at these events. If there is a small container with toothpicks in that is a hint that you are not supposed to take the food with your fingers. There should also be an empty container for used toothpicks, otherwise hold the small piece of wood until you find somewhere discreet to put it.

4. Don't double dip

If a sauce is provided for crudités or shrimp or something similar only dip a fresh piece of food into it. Do not take a bite and then dip again. It's that old saliva worry rearing its head once more.

5. Avoid bores

The best advice I was ever given if attending a cocktail party or a work do on your own – carry two drinks. You will look as though you are en route to deliver a drink to someone and can easily move away from some dullard. If you get stuck, you will at least have plenty to drink.

6. Avoid name-dropping

Name-dropping makes you look like a crawler, as Alan Sugar once told me.

7. Try to keep everything in your left hand

Hold your glass and any napkin or used toothpicks in your left hand so that your right is always free to shake hands. You're there to meet people, remember? If you can't manage to hold everything, stop taking more canapés. Your glass may contain ice, so holding it in your left hand will also stop your right becoming cold and unpleasant to shake hands with.

What else. Oh, I know …

8. What to do with olive stones?

They can be laid on the table if no plate is provided. The easiest thing is to avoid eating them.

9. Know when to leave

Judge your exit carefully. You need to stay long enough to show willing and not so long that you appear entirely friendless outside the office circle. I know, for example, that it's time for me to go now and move on to the next topic.

I only ever worked briefly in an office and I have to say it didn't suit me. When the *New Yorker* magazine was launched in 1925, the publication had no money. The editor Harold Ross had the foresight to hire the genius that was Dorothy Parker, but she didn't always come in to work. One day he demanded an explanation for her absence when there was a piece which needed writing. Parker had a perfectly reasonable excuse: 'Someone else,' she said, 'was using the pencil.'

Work is important not just to earn money. It's often a place where we spend a lot of time and, as a consequence, may well be the place where we meet our significant other. I think you've had enough time on your own so let's go looking for a mate.

Much love

Sandi

8: HAVING RELATIONS

Penguins mate for life. That doesn't surprise me much because they all look alike. It's not like they're going to meet a really new, great looking penguin someday.

Unknown

Dear Mary

It's hard to know the exact order of events in anyone's life until you look back. Embarking on a sexual relationship or, as my biology teacher used to call it, 'having relations', begins for everyone at slightly different times. Ideally it will be when you are mature enough to be able to deal with it and young enough to have the most fun. I think it's one of the great pleasures of life, but there have always been rules about it, probably because everyone has slightly different ideas about what the concept of 'pleasure' entails.

Your choice of partner depends partly on the social code you've been brought up with and quite a lot on your ...

PHEROMONES

Greek this time. *Phero* meaning 'to bear' and *hormone* from the Greek word for 'impetus'. We have quite a lot of these and they are something we have in common with most living things.

Even bacteria have pheromones. The female silk worm secretes something called *bombykol*, a pheromone which makes male moths so horny they will fly long distances to find the female. It's so powerful, and the males become so keen, that you can use tiny quantities of *bombykol* to attract male moths away from an area they are infesting. This only goes to prove that lust can make anyone fail to think straight.

When you fall in love the body and the brain go a little crazy. Some people start sweating, others feel light-headed, the stomach can feel as though it is doing somersaults, it can be hard to think and so on. It is not a good time to be sensible. That doesn't mean, however, that it isn't worth following a few basic principles in the great dating and sex game. Whether these principles represent good manners or good sense is a grey area. Quite often it's a bit of both. You behave well so that the world treats you well.

Now it is popular in books trying to offer some thoughts on behaviour to separate heterosexual and homosexual behaviour, but actually most of the basic principles in having a one-to-one relationship are exactly the same, whatever the combination of genders happens to be. The animal kingdom is full of examples of creatures who move from homosexual to heterosexual behaviour and vice versa without getting overly agitated. If there are specifics for one kind of sexual orientation I'll get to them later.

WHERE DO YOU FIND A MATE?

Sometimes you're just lucky. My favourite story is about another Dane, the opera tenor, Lauritz Melchior. In the 1920s he was working in Munich. He was sitting in a garden learning the words to a new opera. As he sang the words, 'Come to me, my love, on the wings of light,' he said, 'there was a flutter, a flash of white, and there sitting at my feet, was a beautiful little creature who had dropped right out of the blue.' It was Maria Hacker, a silent film star from Bavaria. She had been making a parachute jump for a movie and been blown off course. They married in 1925 and stayed devoted until she passed away in 1963.

Workplace

I've already mentioned being cautious about this. Don't date the boss unless you plan to find work elsewhere, and don't annoy your co-workers by doing nothing but 'making eyes' across the workplace at your beloved.

Social groups

Those looking for a companion are often advised to 'get out more' and join some kind of group. Just remember that other people who have joined the book club, swimming association, ramblers in Rochester or whatever may have joined simply to read, swim or ramble. Be sensitive to the group's needs. A whole group has not been formed just so you can sort out your sex life. This is also true when you meet someone at college or university.

Online dating

Lots of people live alone. In the UK, 34 per cent of households have one person living in them. That's nearly 20 million people. (In Sweden it is 47 per cent, which is an astonishing number of folk playing solitaire.) Some people really like the solo life, but others are looking for a mate. It's now reckoned that about a third of all relationships in the UK start online in an industry worth about £368m per year. It's clearly worth a shot, but it's also worth considering …

When you meet someone online

1. Be yourself

If you have a great photo of yourself in a swimming gala you may want to use this as your profile picture. If, however, the gala took place twenty years ago, this is a really bad idea. You are not offering someone a date, you are proffering disappointment. Give an honest portrait of yourself so that no one's hopes are dashed when you actually meet. This means also being honest about what you do and don't like. Saying you are keen on opera when you have never been could mean sitting through sixteen hours of Wagner's Ring Cycle.

2. Take it slowly

If you blurt out every detail about yourself in a first account

- There will be nothing left to talk about when you meet.

- You will be sharing details with a complete stranger who may not have been entirely honest about themselves in their online description. You don't know them.

- Don't start referring to someone you've only met online as being your boy/girlfriend/partner/fiancée/anything other than 'someone you've only met online and don't actually know at all'. You are living in fantasy land if you think you are in a relationship conducted solely through keystrokes.

Setting up dates for others

Don't make your friend go on a date with your rather tragic brother or sister just because he or she is lonely. If you can't help matchmaking, do it properly. Find out what your friend likes/ dislikes in a mate and spend time trying to think of someone suitable. It's quite a fun game trying to find a date for a friend who really only likes to talk about Etruscan coinage or some other niche interest. If you or they are too busy, you could suggest ...

Speed dating

This is a quick way to meet a lot of other single people. It was invented by a Los Angeles Rabbi called Yaacov Deyo to help young Jewish singles to find a partner. Presumably he felt the traditional route of having your grandmother find you someone was not working as well as it used to. Just because you are meeting a flock of people at speed doesn't mean you shouldn't ...

1. Make an effort

Even if you have a disastrous dating track record give this moment your best shot. Look nice, don't reek of garlic, and smile.

2. Be nice

Even if you decide instantly that someone is not for you, don't just blurt that out. Everyone is nervous. Be respectful and try to be interested. Don't sit yawning or playing on your phone. This is supposed to be fun for everyone.

3. Keep your chin up

This is not the forum to tell a complete stranger what a lousy time you are having or how your ex ruined your life.

4. Accept what is happening

If you really like the look of someone but they are clearly not interested, move on. The gong will sound very soon and who knows how fabulous the next person may turn out to be.

On an actual date

Whenever I date a guy, I think, 'Is this the man I want my children to spend their weekends with?'

Rita Rudner, American comedian

All the rules above apply plus a few new ones:

1. Be open-minded

So you've never been out with an aerospace engineer before, but it's not rocket science … well, obviously it might be but that doesn't mean you can't get on.

2. Put your phone away

Try to be in the room with the person you are seeing. Focus, people!

3. Be yourself

However lonely you are, don't be tempted to put on an act just to please your date. There is going to come a time when you can't keep the pretence up any longer and will have to attend a Formula One race with the petrolhead you find yourself dating.

4. Drinking too much during dinner . . .

If you haven't got the message on this one yet you might want to seek a little counselling.

5. Don't moan or monologue

This is not a therapy session where you speak and someone else is paid to listen.

6. If it went well

Be quick to get back in touch. Trying to be 'cool' never reads well.

7. If it went badly

Give someone a chance. I think there should be at least two dates before you give up on someone, but be honest. If you know from the very beginning that the relationship is going to go nowhere don't just go on a second date to be nice. It will only get more difficult to say you are not interested.

Making conversation

The Victorians had very clear ideas about what men and women might talk about – the weather has been a safe subject for the British since clouds were first invented, but they were also happy to consider improving books, balls (in a party sense), and travel. Talking to someone you don't know can be hard work until you work out areas of mutual interest. If you have asked someone on a date or you have accepted a request for a date, then it would be terrible if you make no effort to chat with the person concerned. Try to make it fun. Luckily there are various areas of common ground other than how you're going to get home.

Good topics

1. Career

There is a reason why the Queen asks everyone 'And what do you do?' when she visits somewhere. It is often a big part of someone's life. If you are a vegetarian and find your date works in an abattoir that may or may not be a helpful sign about your possible future together.

2. Free time

Many people work to live rather than the other way round. How people spend their free time gives you an idea of what they think is important. The person obsessed with participating in triathlons may struggle to date a couch potato who in turn may fail to see the attraction of lycra.

3. Family

Everyone loves talking about themselves. Taking an interest in their background is polite and tells you a great deal about them.

4. Where have you been?

Travel is a nice safe ground where you can find out if the person is a keen globetrotter who loves anything new or someone with a slightly narrower vision who has holidayed in the same B & B on the Isle of Wight since they were a child.

5. Food and drink

We all eat and what we like to eat says quite a lot about us. Foodie or fusspot?

6. Films, books, music

Have you seen …? Have you read … ? Do you like …?

7. The weather

If you are really stuck. I mean, really stuck, or happen to be a weather forecaster.

Schopenhauer's bet

The German philosopher Arthur Schopenhauer (1788–1860) believed that it is a general dissatisfaction with life that drives people forward. He had some pretty dodgy views and concluded his life living in Frankfurt with a succession of pet poodles. He is said to have dined alone quite often in an inn also patronised by English officers. Before each meal, Arthur would put a single gold coin on the table and would leave it there until he had finished, when he would put it back in his pocket. When asked why he did this, he is said to have explained that it was a personal bet with himself. If, during his dinner, he overheard an Englishman talk about anything other than horses, dogs or women, he would give the money to the poor.

Dodgy topics

1. The past

Everyone has baggage and it's best not to try to open it up on early dates. There will be plenty of time for unpacking later.

2. Politics

Don't have a row on your first date.

3. Religion

Again, can cause trouble.

4. Anything too weird or too geeky

Unless you actually met at an IT support conference or a Star Trek convention, maybe keep your more niche interests to yourself until later. I know I said you should be honest, but maybe introduce anything oddball a little slowly. By then the person may like you enough not to find you odd.

MEN ON DATES WITH WOMEN

Sexual Organs of Men – carry your sexual organs towards the left thigh where nature makes the largest place for them.

Orson Squire Fowler, *Creative and Sexual Science: or Manhood, Womanhood, and their Mutual Interrelations… as taught by Phrenology and Physiology* (1875)

Mary, just so you know – boys are lovely. I have a boy of my own, but sometimes they need a little extra guidance so this bit is for them. Boys –

1. Make an effort

You don't have to have a lot of money to show someone a good time. If you can't afford a restaurant then you could cook or make a picnic. This is really one of those occasions mothers often bang on about when 'it's the thought that counts'. Try to find out what your date is interested in and tailor an event accordingly. There are a lot of things you can do which cost nothing at all.

It is also OK to share the costs of a date but you need to think this through. We all like a treat and perhaps offering to pay would be nice. If you want to 'go Dutch' make sure this is really clear well before you go out. Mentioning it as the bill arrives is not going to go well.

2. The rutting boar

Don't overdo the aftershave. You are not a rutting boar whose scents need masking from hunters.

3. The ruddy bore

All the usual caveats about conversation apply. Try to make the date about the woman you are spending the evening with. You never know, she may be interesting as well as attractive. Try to vary your conversation. You may even find you like yourself better.

4. Mind your language

Really? Am I going to be so dreary as to suggest a boy should mind his Ps and Qs on a date? Well, yes. Here's a little tip, boys – women are suckers for a man who appears to be a gentleman. Speak nicely, don't swear and don't launch into jokes you would tell at a rugby dinner.

5. Mind your . . . you know, don't you? . . . alcohol consumption

No one wants to see that you haven't yet managed to grow up.

WOMEN ON DATES WITH MEN

There was a general whisper, toss, and wiggle,
But etiquette forbade them all to giggle.

Lord Byron, *Don Juan*: Canto the Fifth

Dating has changed a lot and it is possible for a woman to ask a man out although it still seems oddly rare. Why the ball is so often in the male court is hard to say. If you are a woman who fancies a fellow then you can suggest having 'a drink sometime' or invite them to an event which isn't strictly speaking simply a date – the theatre, cinema, a party and so on. I don't think this imbalance about who asks who should exist, but the fact is it seems to.

Once you are on a date consider a few matters:

1. He's not from Mars

You can find plenty of books that tell you that the sexes view each other as alien beings. We're constantly told that women speak more, emote more, while men struggle with their feelings and prefer action; that men and women communicate differently. Oxford language professor Deborah Cameron believes this is a myth and so do I. I think it's astonishingly patronising to men to decide they can only speak in grunts, most of which are to do with sex. As Professor Cameron says of the 'Men are from Mars' genre of writing about the sexes '… why do men put up with books that put them on a par with Lassie or Skippy the

Bush Kangaroo ("Hey, wait a minute – I think he's trying to tell us something!")?'

The widely publicised notion that women use three times as many words in a day as men is just nonsense. There are no studies to back this up.

Don't presume the man in front of you is not capable of very intense and interesting conversation. He is not a Neanderthal. He's just like you but with different dress sense. Look for the similarities not the differences.

2. Consider the finances

If you are on a date where the man is clearly paying, think twice before you order the most expensive items. Be kind to his wallet – offer to share or to pay next time.

GETTING PHYSICAL

Two young women from Staffordshire visited him when I was present, to consult him on the subject of Methodism, to which they were inclined. 'Come, (said he,) you pretty fools, dine with Maxwell and me at the Mitre, and we will talk over that subject'; which they did, and after dinner he took one of them upon his knee, and fondled her for half an hour together.

The Life of Samuel Johnson (1791) by James Boswell.

If all has gone well on a date then you may be ready to move on …

Kissing

Kissing has been a popular, free and non-fattening pastime for years. The first kiss ever seen in the movies was in William Heise's silent screen film, *The Kiss*, whose title was a bit of a clue to the content. It was shot in 1896 and featured May Irwin and John C. Rice in a controversial clinch. The short spool caused an uproar with American publisher Herbert S. Stone, who called the film 'absolutely disgusting' and demanded 'police interference'. He stormed, 'Neither participant is physically attractive and the spectacle of their prolonged pasturing on each other's lips was hard to bear.' Kissing is less controversial these days but still bears a little examination.

The joy of osculation

Philematology is the science of kissing while osculation is the kissing itself. Try as I might, I have not found a single professional philematologist to give you kissing facts, but there is the odd biologist who will. It's from them we get confirmation of the fact that on the whole men are sloppier kissers. Apparently (and you may not want to think about this) saliva has testosterone in it. Biologists suggest men are keener on the sloppy, open-mouthed kiss because they are unconsciously trying to arouse the woman with their hormones. It is also thought that men use kissing to initiate sex while women like it afterwards. Whenever it happens, here are a few guidelines ...

Osculation orders
Do

1. Brush your teeth
No one is attracted by halitosis. If they are, you might want to look at other issues they have before you push the boat out towards further contact. If you can't brush your teeth at least get a mint.

2. Take it slowly
A first kiss should always be gentle. You are checking out the terrain and shouldn't ride roughshod over it.

3. Breathe
Gasping for air during a kiss suggests the action has been life-threatening.

4. Be sensitive

It isn't all about your own needs. Be alert to how the other person is feeling and whether they want to carry on. Allegedly the world's longest kiss took place in Thailand between Nontawat Jaroeng-sornsinpose and Thanakorn Sittiamthong. It lasted for fifty hours, twenty-five minutes and a single second. This is unlikely to have been their first date.

5. Smile when you are done

Smiling after a kiss suggests it was a pleasure. Wiping your hand across your mouth suggests it wasn't.

Don't

1. Wipe your hand across your mouth

2. Kiss someone without warning

This is in the school of 'It's New Year's Eve and I have to kiss someone, oh, you'll do' kind of kissing. Everyone deserves some warning that you are heading in on their lips. James Bond movies teach men that if they are good-looking, any woman will welcome their advances without warning. This is not true.

3. Be weird

There are many forms of sexual pleasure and it's not my place to comment on them. Just a tip – if you lick someone else's teeth during a first kiss they may not like it.

Cataglottism

The kiss is not only an expression of feeling; it is a means of provoking it. Cataglottism is by no means confined to pigeons.

Havelock Ellis, *Studies in the Psychology of Sex*,1927.

It means kissing using the tongue. It used to be known as 'French kissing'. Who knew that pigeons do it? Anyway, you need to know someone very well to think this is a good idea. It is never a good idea on a first kiss. I'm going to be crystal clear – don't ram your tongue in someone's mouth unless you are absolutely sure it is what is wanted.

SEX

Having sex with someone is often the next step after dating. If it comes before dating then you probably won't be seeking behavioural guidance from a book. There are plenty of other places to look for advice on this subject so I'll keep it brief.

For some people it is a step accomplished quickly, while others take a bit more time. The Victorians heartily disapproved of pre-marital sex but that's not to say it didn't happen. When I was a little girl in the 1960s my grandmother used to volunteer at a psychiatric hospital. In it were two very elderly sisters who had been there all their lives. Their only issue had been being born 'the wrong side of the blanket' to Victorian aristocracy.

Being intimate with someone is a big deal and ideally it needs to be given quite a lot of thought, so there's a little bit of serious stuff to get out of the way.

1. No pressure
No one has to share their body with another living soul if they don't want to.

2. Have a wash
This probably doesn't seem that serious but seriously, no one is going to want to exchange fluids with you if you are on the high side. Even if your potential partner is clearly receptive, take a minute to have a once over. It will be worth it.

3. Be playful
No one likes a boring lover. Anything repeated over and over again can be tiresome. I have a small book published in the 1600s which talks about sex in terms of food. How can I put this? No

one wants to eat the same thing at every meal. It's also worth checking that you are enjoying the meal at a suitable time and place.

4. Be sensitive

In the movies, ripping someone's clothes off can look great. In reality it's expensive. The amount of physical horseplay a couple gets up to has to be mutually agreeable. Forcing someone to do something they don't like is just wrong. Just because you have a fantasy does not mean it is shared. See if you can't have some new flights of fancy together. In order to do that you will, of course, need to …

5. Focus

Comes up a lot, doesn't it? Taking a phone call in the middle of sex may not go down well.

6. After-play

Foreplay gets quite a lot of publicity but after-play is equally important. Very few people are 100 per cent confident about either their bodies or their performance. Getting straight up after sex with no thought for the other person makes them feel horrible, so don't. Please clean up after yourself. No one wants to find a used prophylactic lying about. This is especially true if you are staying at your partner's parents' place. Probably the worst thing you can say after sex? 'Sorry, what was your name again?'

Protection plans

The *Kahun Gynaecological Papyrus* is the oldest known medical text of any kind. Dated to about 180 BC, it recommends crocodile dung as a contraceptive. If that was too much, a pessary of sour milk, honey with a pinch of natron (you can find it in saline lake beds) and acacia gum was just fine instead.

This is a topic that requires discussion between the two people involved. It is not simply the woman's problem. I knew a very distinguished journalist who once moaned to me, 'My girlfriend has only gone and got herself pregnant.' 'Really?' I said, 'and where were you at the time?'

Condom curiosity

During the Second World War, British soldiers had problems with gun barrels either corroding near the sea or icing up in the winter. They solved this by putting a condom over the gun's barrel. The system was such a success at keeping artillery dry that it was decided larger weapons might benefit from something similar. It was suggested to the then prime minister Winston Churchill that condom manufacturers might make some 18-inch condoms. He agreed on one condition: the new 'rubbers' had to have two labels – one reading 'For Use By British Servicemen'; and the second reading 'Small'.

Health warning

Be safe. (It's like a sexual mantra, isn't it?) Don't tell someone you are healthy if you don't know. You may not know the truth about yourself. It's very hard to tell if someone has an STI. About 70 per cent of women and 50 per cent of men with chlamydia have no symptoms. Don't say 'I love you' just to make someone have sex without protection. Don't say using protection affects your performance, your pleasure or anything else that will force someone to have sex without protection. Emotional blackmail is not nice.

Old sexual words you might care to revive

From the *Dictionary of the Vulgar Tongue, A Dictionary of Buckish Slang, University Wit and Pickpocket Elegance*, compiled by Captain Grose (1811):

Apple Dumpling Shop: A woman's bosom.

Blind Cupid: The backside.

Detumescence: The act of subsiding from a swollen state, especially the relaxation of an erect penis. It's the same as 'flaccid' except that 'flaccid' sounds more, well, flaccid.

Green Gown: To give a girl a green gown; to tumble her on the grass.

Riding St George: The woman uppermost in the amorous congress, that is, the dragon upon St George. This is said to be the way to get a bishop.

Rantallion: One whose scrotum is so relaxed as to be longer than his penis, i.e. whose shot pouch is longer than the barrel of his piece. (Really?)

That will do.

COMMITMENT

At seventeen, most of our belles of fashion expect to receive proposals. If they do not marry within a few years after their introduction, they have a mortified sense of having lost time – that the expectations of friends and of parents have not been fulfilled; that others have 'gone off' before them.

Florence Hartley, The Ladies' Book of Etiquette, and Manual of Politeness, 1872

There was a time when royals got married at all ages. Isabella of Valois married Richard II of England when she was just six. These days this would be frowned upon. In the UK there is no set age for marriage, civil partnership or co-habiting, apart from the legal age for these commitments being eighteen without parental consent and sixteen with. It is unusual these days for a commitment ceremony to take place before there has been a period of living together. Co-habiting is accepted as a good way to ensure that a long-lasting partnership has been created. About 5.9 million people co-habit in the UK today, a figure that has doubled in less than twenty years.

Paraphernalia

These days we think of paraphernalia as just 'stuff' but it's
actually an old family law term meaning 'things beyond the
dowry'. The Romans started it with a legal concept of property
which a married woman owned and which didn't form part of
her dowry. Usually it was things such as clothing and jewellery
which she was allowed to keep for herself whatever happened.
Many men may not be surprised to learn that, strictly speaking,
only women can have paraphernalia.

Co-habiting

Moving in with someone means you have agreed to be a team.
You may have lived with your family or on your own for some
time and it can be difficult to adjust. There are a few simple ways
to ease into a partnership.

1. Make some space

If your partner is moving into a place where you have been living
on your own, make sure there is some room for them. They may
not want to hang around if they're not even allowed a mug for
their toothbrush.

2. Don't be a fascist

This is generally a good rule in life, but is particularly useful when
it comes to learning to live together. It is possible that you adore
furniture and cushions with mad, floral decorations. It is also
possible that your new partner thinks this style would only suit
a great-aunt opening a bordello. You need to discuss the home
environment and find a decor that you can both live with.

3. Remember you are in a partnership

If you receive an invitation to attend something on your own,
discuss it with your partner. Just heading off to a social event by
yourself may make them feel anxious and you won't be popular

when you get back. If you don't want to share your life, you could always live alone. Swings and roundabouts.

4. Household chores

Hardly anyone enjoys housework, yet housework is a running sore in most of our lives. You need to share the chores. Discuss it. No one is moving in so that you don't have to do laundry. Discuss who is doing what or who is going to pay for it. A study in the US found that after faithfulness and a good sex life, sharing household chores was listed as the third most popular factor for a happy marriage. If men need encouraging, remind them about the modern concept of 'chore play'. This is where a man tries 'to seduce his wife by completing menial tasks around the home which she would usually perform herself'. Apparently it works.

5. Privacy

Just because your partner's post now lands on the doormat doesn't mean you are entitled to open it. Ideally partners shouldn't have secrets, but everyone is entitled to a little wriggle room in deciding what to share and when. Bank statements, letters, diaries, computers – these are all areas where you need to respect privacy.

6. Keep confidences

Partnerships need to be based on trust. If your partner tells you something in confidence then you must keep the secret. If you don't, they may never tell you anything again.

7. Be supportive

Don't criticise your partner in front of other people. Keep it buttoned till you get home. The old adage of not washing your dirty linen in public is a good one. Honesty is good, but sometimes best practised at home.

8. Family and friends

No one arrives without having had a life before. Being rude to your partner's family or friends is a comment on their previous life. Don't. Accept the person you have fallen for with all their attendants. If you really don't like someone from their past, make space for your partner to see them alone. Try to accept that your partner may not see a shining glow around all of your folks.

9. Exes

Some people maintain very close relationships with previous partners. Make sure you discuss this, so that your present partner does not feel like some sort of also-ran.

10. Children

Hopefully it won't be a surprise to you if your new partner has children from a previous relationship. You will have no choice but to accept them into your life. If you do not want children, then do not have a relationship with this person. It's not fair on the kids.

Good lord, what a lot of things to think about. Well, if you can crack that, then you may fancy a more formal stage …

MARRIAGE/MORE COMMITMENT

A man is never well settled in the saddle of his fortunes until he be married.

George Routledge (1812–88), *Routledge's Manual of Etiquette*

There was a time when marriage was a rather unbalanced contract between a man and a woman. She gave him all her property, which he was free to dispose of as he pleased, and in exchange she lost all rights over her own body. He could divorce her for adultery, while she just had to put up with his philandering. Fortunately things have improved since then. Marriage can be great. The American comedian Jack Benny and his wife Mary Livingstone were married from 1927 until his death in 1974. In his will Benny stipulated that a single red rose should be delivered to his wife every day of her remaining life.

The proposal

It used to be up to the man alone whether he wanted 'to enshrine so precious a gem in the casket of his affections' (*Routledge's Manual of Etiquette*) by asking a woman to marry him. The trouble with proposals is that the very topic is weighed down by fairy tales and fantasies. Many women, even feisty feminists, may still have a dream about a man getting down on one knee and asking for her hand. If you are a traditionalist then the man has to do the asking or he will feel emasculated. It's a ritual in which a man makes a grand gesture. Let's be frank, however. With most of the heterosexual couples I have come across, what happens is that the woman makes it very clear that the relationship has reached the stage where the man needs to propose. He then takes his time, makes her crazy and finally gets on with it.

The traditional man asks woman

1. Don't jump the gun

Be sure this is what the woman you are seeing wants. Excellent clues include – living together, her talking a lot about marriage and casually reading wedding magazines. Do not ask a woman to marry you if you have only just met. It works in the movies but rarely in real life. Having said that do also ...

2. Get on with it

Consider the tale told by Henry Longfellow in his poem, *The Courtship of Miles Standish*. Standish was one of the pilgrims on *The Mayflower* which set sail for Cape Cod in 1620. According to Longfellow, Standish was a man among men but a dribbling wreck around women. He fell in love with a fellow passenger, a young girl from Dorking called Priscilla Mullens, but he was afraid to speak up so he asked the ship's carpenter, John Alden, to do it for him. Well, you can guess what happened. Alden married Mullens.

The characters in the story are real but the love triangle may not be. Nevertheless, don't take a chance on losing the one you love.

3. The ring

You don't have to have one. She may want to choose her own. Be very sure you have good taste before choosing jewellery for a woman which she is going to have to wear every day for the rest of her life.

4. Make it memorable

Hopefully this is a one-off event. If you think it might not be, then you need to consider whether she is the one for you. Choosing a romantic location is nice. Remember you are showing the woman of your dreams how much you love her (plus all her friends will want details of every single thing that happened). Making an effort to make the moment perfect for her is essential. Just because you are a big Arsenal fan does not mean she wants to be proposed to at half-time at The Emirates. In fact in general ...

5. Avoid public proposals

Hard as it may be to believe, it is possible the woman does not want to marry you. It is unfair on your potential partner to put the extra pressure of an audience on her decision. Don't start a marriage on the basis of anyone being too embarrassed to turn you down. Being refused publicly is awful for everyone – the person asking, the person asked and the poor members of the public who don't know where to look when the woman walks off. YouTube has any number of cringe-inducing video examples of men being refused on basketball courts and in food courts. In fact, courts in general seem a poor choice.

6. A refusal

It does happen. Don't panic. Talk to her. Maybe your loved one needs more time.

7. Asking her father for her hand?

This is a patriarchal tradition which on the surface may upset the modern women. It can, however, simply be seen as a way of showing respect towards her family and may be a nice gesture.

Do this after she has said yes. Everyone needs to understand that it is not actually the father's decision. It's a game. A nice game.

29th February

This date occurs once every four years and was designed to balance the calendar. According to tradition it is also the day that a woman can ask a man to marry her. The notion was said to have started in fifth-century Ireland when St Bridget had a chat with St Patrick about women having to wait for so long for a man to propose and he suggested once every four years would be enough. Folklore suggests a man who refuses such a proposal has to pay a fine of a silk dress or a pair of gloves.

The Americans have a similar pseudo-serious day called Sadie Hawkins Day on 15 November. It arose from the comic strip *Li'l Abner*, and again it's the one time when women supposedly take charge of proposals.

Homosexual partnerships

It is up to the couple how much like a heterosexual betrothal they want to make it. Who asks who depends on the dynamic in the relationship. Most of the above applies, and checking that your partner's family is happy with it all is a nice touch.

PLANNING THE WEDDING/CIVIL PARTNERSHIP

The only important thing about a wedding/civil partnership or any commitment ceremony is that it is an occasion which properly celebrates the couple getting hitched. There is no such thing as a 'proper' wedding. You cannot go wrong if vows are taken and everyone has a good time.

Pre-nup agreements

These are popular but seem to me rather poor form. Having a

legal arrangement about what you will do if you split up rather suggests you are hedging your bets in the first place. There is a rather fine judge in Pennsylvania called J. Michael Eakin who is given to delivering his verdicts in verse. In 2002 he was sitting in judgment on Porreco v Porreco. Susan Porreco claimed that her husband Louis had defrauded her because the engagement ring she thought to be a diamond worth $21,000 was in fact a worthless cubic zirconia. She believed this lie should void their prenuptial agreement. Eakins ruled for Susan saying,

> A groom must expect matrimonial pandemonium
> When his spouse finds he's given her a cubic zirconium
> Instead of a diamond in her engagement band
> The one he said was worth twenty-one grand.

The case battled on to the Supreme Court where Susan lost. According to the court, Susan should have checked the ring out herself before she married him.

If you think the relationship may not last, then maybe don't get married at all. If, however, you are confident about the commitment then let's get cracking. Weddings don't organise themselves …

The location

Try to be nice to all your guests. It may be that it is your dream to tie the knot underwater in the Maldives, but consider the cost to everyone who wants to come. This is your big day, but if you are planning to share it with your loved ones then a little consideration would be appreciated. That doesn't mean you need to have the wedding anyone else wants for you either. It's supposed to be a day of joy for everyone.

The theme

Same again. Consider how everyone you invite might feel about attending anything dressed as a Teletubby.

Who should be invited?

The first thing is to work out where you are having the event and how many people you can afford to invite. Then you need to make a list. That should be the easy bit, but you may stumble on …

The theory of relativity

This can be a nightmare, so you really need to want to be together.

Unless you are getting married in a registry office with just the minimum two witnesses (which has its advantages) then you need to start with all your closest relatives – parents, siblings, grandparents, etc. Ideally you don't want to leave out any relatives, but it depends how big your family is and what you can afford. If you cannot invite everyone, then you should at least let them know that it is because of cost. Write a nice letter explaining the situation and saying how sorry you are not to ask them. You never know, they might offer to pay for something. Perhaps leave out relatives who disapprove of your partner, lifestyle or general behaviour. This is not a day to have someone tutting every time you move.

Do invite friends

Make sure you pick real friends and not people you feel you 'ought' to invite but who you haven't seen for years. It is, however, a very special occasion so there may well be people you don't see regularly who you would still like to have attend. It is also fine to invite some people to the party afterwards and not to the ceremony.

Don't invite friends …

who you only know through Facebook.

Do invite co-workers

Don't feel you have to invite everyone from your place of work. If you don't usually socialise with them you don't have to invite them to your wedding. Suggest an after-hours drink instead to mark the occasion.

Don't invite co-workers ...

because you think it will improve your chances of promotion at work. This is supposed to be a romantic occasion, not a networking opportunity.

Don't invite people you don't know

This probably seems a lunatic thing to say. Of course you wouldn't invite someone you don't know, but it could happen. Someone you invite may want to bring a date who you don't know. This is not necessary and it is fine to say there just isn't room. However, do be flexible. If someone is going to know hardly anyone at the event but you want them there (an old school chum, say) then it might be nice to let them bring someone to talk to. Who knows, it could be the start of a beautiful friendship.

Most important

Once you have invited someone you cannot change your mind. If people say they can't make it, leave it at that.

The ceremony

It is possible to go too far with these things. Katie Holmes and Tom Cruise, David Gest and Liza Minnelli, Paul McCartney and Heather Mills? What do they all have in common? They all spent millions on their weddings, oh and ... well, it didn't work out that brilliantly. It's about love, not about how lavish the event is. The degree of formality depends on whether there is an existing structure to the event such as a religious element. You can make the ceremony what you wish, although there are legal formalities which have to be adhered to. There are entire books devoted to every nuance of wedding planning so I shan't be too detailed. Suffice to say there are some ...

Basic rules for guests

I'm sure you're ahead of me by now so I don't need to tell you to:

- Arrive clean and neat.
- Don't be drunk (of course).
- Don't cry and say it should have been you.
- Don't shout out when the person officiating asks if there are any impediments, however tempting it may be. (Although it's very entertaining if you can persuade a child to do this.)

Gifts

If you are worried about a wedding gift, consider the story in the Old Testament when David wanted to marry the king's daughter, Michal. Apparently the king requested 'no marriage present except a hundred foreskins of the Philistines'. David went and got them. I have no idea how he might have wrapped them. Still, full marks for being so resourceful. Foreskins fail to appear on most gift lists so whatever you buy for someone, it has to be less unpleasant.

The vows

The words 'Honour and Obey' must also be distinctly spoken by the bride. They constitute an essential part of the obligation and contract of matrimony on her part.

George Routledge (1812–88), *Routledge's Manual of Etiquette*

No they don't.

Apart from the most formal part of a religious or civil ceremony, you can write the vows yourselves. Make sure the words reflect what you both feel.

After the ceremony – the happy couple

1. Do remember your partner as you party

The person you just married? It's why you're there.

2. Make time for everyone

Ensure that everyone invited gets a private word with you. Some people may have come a long way and everyone has worried about what to wear.

3. Make speeches pleasant

This is not a time for anyone to show off about bachelor/single life exploits. Try to thank everyone, including the parents.

4. Forget the ex

Now is not the time to even mention the name of a past love.

5. Be thrilled with everything

Don't moan about the quality of your presents.

6. Forget about the cost

It's too late now.

7. Be grateful

Make sure you send thank-you notes to everyone who came. Ideally these should not be text messages, emails or Facebook postings. Handwritten is nicest.

After the ceremony – the guests

1. Be delighted and delightful

Don't moan about the food, the venue or your seat at the table. Don't comment unfavourably on anyone's clothing, physical appearance or manner. You may have no idea which side of the family you are offending.

2. Forget the past

Don't sob loudly in a way that suggests regret or say that you used to go out with one half of the couple. Never say you've slept with them both even if it's true.

If you can avoid all these things you should have a very jolly time.

GAY'S THE WORD

According to the Office for National Statistics, 1.5 per cent of the British population is gay. People who are homophobic have a fear of 1.5 per cent of everyone they meet. Often they worry that homosexuals can 'promote' same-sex life – 'Hello, I'm a homosexual. Would you like a two-week trial of our lifestyle? You receive this free carriage clock, yours to keep whatever you decide.' Or they worry that heterosexuals who meet homosexuals will be 'converted'. To me this suggests a fragility to heterosexuality which seems surprising.

If you think you haven't met a homosexual before then you are almost certainly mistaken, but here are a few tips. It is common these days to lump lesbians, gay men, bisexuals and transsexuals all under one umbrella known as LGBT people. This does not mean that all lesbians, gay men, bisexuals and transsexuals lead their lives in exactly the same way, but there are …

A few occasional and odd heterosexual assumptions

1. I am the same sex as the gay person so they must fancy me

Don't assume a gay person is coming on to you. Just because you are the same sex as a homosexual does not mean they fancy you. Most homosexuals fancy other homosexuals. Don't flatter yourself.

2. Gay people have a lot of sex. Bisexuals must have even more

Don't assume anything about anyone's sex life. You may think LGBT people spend more time having sex than straight people but generally all people, whatever their sexuality, spend an astonishing amount of time with their partner on dull things such as wondering whether the milk has gone off. Just because you know someone is gay does not mean you are free to ask them detailed questions about their sex life.

3. Lesbians hate men
They don't. They just don't want to share body fluid with them.

4. It's a 'lifestyle choice'
It isn't.

5. It's easy to spot an LGBT person
It isn't. Just like heterosexuals, LGBT people are available in every shape, type and size. The phrases 'You're too pretty to be a lesbian'; 'too manly to be gay', and suchlike, never go well.

On the whole

1. Use the right language
Don't say – queer, fag, dyke, homo, poofter, trannie, queen, 'batting for the other team' or anything else which might be offensive. If you are not sure how to refer to a couple, follow their lead. Some say partner, some say boyfriend, husband, wife, girlfriend.

2. Let people 'out' themselves
It is not your place to tell anyone how to live their life. Coming out is an entirely personal matter.

3. Be sensitive
There are still too many LGBT people who are abandoned by their families once they come out. Don't go on about your own brilliant family if your LGBT friend is having problems.

4. Don't stare if you see a gay couple hold hands
Take a test for yourself and see how much heterosexual couple imagery you see in a day – on television, in magazines, on bill-boards. It is everywhere, so to same-sex people, holding hands is honestly a drop in the ocean of sexual behaviour.

5. Don't presume gay parents are any different to other parents

Kids need love and attention. That's it. Every study ever done on the subject shows that kids brought up by gay parents grow up just like any other kids and can be just as annoying.

If someone comes out to you

Why is it that, as a culture, we are more comfortable seeing two men holding guns than holding hands?

Ernest Gaines, African American author (born 1933)

1. Don't ask how they know or if they are sure

If you are heterosexual you probably know instinctively. No one ever asks if you're sure. Homosexuals are just like you, but with a smaller range of available partners.

2. Don't be anxious

The gay person is not planning to have sex in front of you.

3. Don't say how fine you are with gay people or that you have a cousin who is gay

It's patronising and no one cares. (You do know what patronising means, don't you?)

4. Don't use the word 'gay' as a put-down

Irritatingly for the homophobe, homosexuals are often very successful. Although 30 per cent of the 'straight' population hold managerial or professional positions, in the gay community it's 49 per cent. Among the great and the good you find an astonishing number of LGBT folk – think artists, Leonardo da Vinci and Michelangelo, or singers, Ma Rainey, the mother of the blues, and Tracy Chapman. There was Hadrian who built that great wall, the writer Christopher Marlowe, and Christina, the Swedish queen.

5. Don't ask if you can watch them having sex

Shouldn't have to write it, should I? You'd be amazed how often it comes up. Mind you, watching others have sex has historical precedence …

Tonight's the night

Catherine de Medici was born in 1519 in Florence, Italy. She was from a prominent and rich family and in 1533 she was taken to France, aged just fourteen, to marry Prince Henry, second son of Francis I, king of France. Henry was also fourteen and once the grand wedding was over the couple retired to their bedroom to consummate the matter. This might have been tough enough for young teenagers who didn't really know each other, but Henry's dad, the king, came to watch, and Pope Clement VII popped in the following morning to see it had all gone well.

Note to heterosexuals attending their first civil partnership

The Bible contains six admonishments to homosexuals and 362 admonishments to heterosexuals. That doesn't mean that God doesn't love heterosexuals. It's just that they need more supervision.

Lynn Lavner, American comedian (1992)

It's two adults declaring their love for each other. It's not scary at all and you will quickly get the hang of what to do. It's just like a wedding except the couple have more chromosomes in common. Don't patronise the couple by ensuring everyone knows how 'liberal' you feel that you are being in attending.

While we're talking about being liberal I should deal with a tricky subject.

Man marries goat

When you are writing a book of suggestions for modern life it is hard to know where to draw the line in the presumptions one makes about basic behaviour. I would have thought …

Don't have sex with animals

was a bit of a given but perhaps I am being naïve. Animals can't give consent so you have to leave them alone, no matter how much you feel they are leading you on.

In 2006, a Sudanese man called Charles Tombe was caught having sex with a goat. The village elders decided that, as he had already used the goat as his 'wife', he had to marry the poor creature and pay a 'dowry' to the owner. The goat, who became known as 'Rose', sadly died the following year when she choked on a plastic bag. She left behind a four-month-old kid. Good manners prevent me from having made any enquiries as to paternity.

There are other examples of animal–human marriages. In 2005 a British woman called Sharon Tendler 'married' a male dolphin called Cindy in Israel. Sadly Cindy passed away the following year. Other ceremonies include men marrying dogs and women marrying snakes or frogs. As far as I can discover no human has married an insect, a fish or a spider. Where would the ring go?

When you go scuba-diving there is something called the 'buddy' system. Every diver pairs up with another and is expected to spend every moment under the water making sure their 'buddy' is all right. Be great if all life were like that. The important thing to recall is that you don't have to marry in order to have it. The great American civil rights campaigner Susan B. Anthony (1820–1906) did not marry herself, but she once wrote 'Marriage, to women as to men, must be a luxury, not a necessity; an incident of life, not all of it.' Have relationships because they enrich your life, not because they are your life. They can be hard work but it is a wonderful thing to have someone who is on your side.

Much love

Sandi

9: LITTLE ONES

Dear Mary

I suspect you won't recall your own entry into the world but we all, rich and poor, aristocrat and peasant, Democrat, Republican, Tory, Labour and even Liberal Democrat arrive in the same way – with no manners at all. Babies often arrive late at night, they scream incessantly and then poo all over you. As St Augustine is said to have remarked, 'Inter urinas et faeces nascimur'. Sorry, I said no Latin, didn't I? 'We are born between urine and faeces', which is not a pleasant thought for anyone.

Whatever domestic set-up they arrive in, and there are a wide variety, babies all head toward life via roughly the same route. Rather like a film from the 1950s, we are now going to imagine that intercourse has taken place and that the pregnancy is under way. (The book *Manners in a Nutshell* published in 1953 doesn't even mention pregnancy although it does answer the important air travel question – 'When the hostess is busy, may a person ask the co-pilot an emergency question?' The answer is no.)

PREGNANCY

These days working out that you are pregnant is as easy as weeing on a stick. Pregnancy tests were a little trickier in the past. Ancient Egyptian women used to have to relieve themselves first on a bag of wheat and then on one of barley. If wheat sprouted, it was a girl. If barley did, it was a boy. If both the bags remained the same (apart from being inedible) there was no pregnancy. (As it happens women's urine does make wheat and barley grow faster which is not a good thought while enjoying certain cereals.)

Throughout history babies have arrived in the same amount of time and in the same manner. It has always taken about nine months and usually involved a degree of pain for the woman involved. What has changed is society's attitude.

> Those who have not been accustomed to bathing should not begin the practice during pregnancy... Foot baths are always dangerous. Sea bathing sometimes causes miscarriage...
> Women of a lymphatic temperament and of a relaxed habit of body are always injured by the bath.
>
> *The Physical Life of Woman: Advice to the Maiden, Wife and Mother*
> by Dr George H. Napheys, 1872

I'm not sure to what degree we might wish to follow George's advice today. He also recommended the application of a puppy to flat nipples in preparation for breastfeeding. What it does tell us, though, is that pregnancy has always been seen as something of a marvel and many folk are not entirely sure how to cope with it. So let's start with some simple basics:

Never ask a woman if she is pregnant

No matter how much a woman may look pregnant it is possible that she is either ill or fat or had a baby quite a while ago and has yet to regain her figure. Never enquire how pregnant someone is unless you absolutely know that they are in the club. Of course, if the woman is enormous you could find yourself in the awkward position of saying nothing and having her believe you think she is fat. The best thing to say is a simple 'How are you?' This general opening leaves the woman free to direct the conversation by either replying 'Fine' or beginning to tell you in some detail about the swelling of her ankles.

(There is a wonderful story about Winston Churchill's best

friend, F. E. Smith, the Earl of Birkenhead. It is said that he was teasing the Lord Chief Justice, Gordon Hewart, about the size of his stomach and asked him whether he was expecting a boy or a girl. 'I don't know,' replied Hewart. 'If it's a boy, I'll call him John,' he declared, 'and if it's a girl I'll call her Mary. But if, as I suspect, it's only wind, I'll call it F. E. Smith!')

When someone tells you that they are pregnant

The first thing is to presume that they are pleased and not to ask 'Did it happen on purpose?' On the whole it is better to let the pregnant person provide you with whatever additional information they choose. If they are not pleased or the father of the child is someone unexpected, let them offer the news. It's not that long ago that having a child out of wedlock carried with it terrible social stigma, but fortunately the world has moved on. If your friend is single don't ask her if she intends to 'tie the knot'. Again, this is a private matter which she will share with you if she chooses. We don't live in the 1950s.

THE PREGNANT WOMAN
Who should you tell?

If a woman has a partner with whom she is happily having the baby then it would be odd not to tell them first. If she doesn't tell her partner first, then perhaps they need to sit down and have a chat about more general matters. After that it rather depends on how quickly the couple would like the news spread. Telling the grandparents-to-be may be lovely but they may not be able to keep it to themselves. Make sure no one important to you is left out of the circle of news and hurt because you didn't consider it important to share with them.

When should you tell?

Some women can't wait to share the news while others are more cautious. The rate for miscarriages drops after the first trimester and some mothers-to-be feel it is safer to make the announcement when they have passed the three month mark. Some, however, may feel that they might cope better with a pregnancy loss if they already had a circle of family and friends who were in the know and would support them.

Of course there will come a time when the pregnant woman will be so pregnant that she will appear not so much to be making new wardrobe choices as wearing an actual wardrobe. At this point who needs to be told becomes somewhat academic.

How should you tell?

This is very big news and a woman may want to consider the best way to spread the word. If the pregnancy is not welcome or a surprise, then anyone the woman tells, particularly, perhaps, the father, may need a little time to think about it. If a woman plans to tell a man by text that she is pregnant it's best if she makes absolutely sure she has the right number.

Dealing with a pregnant woman – Hurrah for hormones

The woman will go through changes over which she has no control. Accept the whims and oddities that go with that. My then partner, six months pregnant, once woke me during a night-time passage on a ferry in the middle of the North Sea demanding tomatoes. Trust me, I knew what was good for me, I found some. Princess Diana, whilst visiting a Cornish fish market in 1989 revealed, 'Everyone was pleased when William was born. I love fish, particularly kippers. I ate them all the time when I was pregnant. They made the house stink …'

A few other basics:

1. Be cheerful

Those people who are already parents and are at the stage where they are not getting enough sleep may be tempted to declare 'Well, that's the end of any good times for you'. This is unfair. Let the newly pregnant person enjoy this moment and discover for themselves that this is the end of good times. If everyone knew the truth about bringing up kids there would be no babies at all. If you have had a baby yourself now is not the time to start warning about morning sickness, birth pain or how your sex life has never returned to normal. Shaking your head over an expectant mother's ruined career prospects is not helpful either.

2. No comment

If the woman is heavily pregnant then she already feels like a barrage balloon tethered to the ground only by her fat ankles. Don't tell her she looks 'ready to pop' as she then might. It's also not advisable to point out any possible mood swings as this will only make them worse.

Don't start commenting on the pregnant person's drinking or smoking or eating. You are probably not a doctor and even if you were, it is not up to you. It's also not polite to the more mature mother-to-be if you comment 'Aren't you a bit old?' In the Biblical story of Moses, his mother, Yocheved, seems to have been 130 when her son was born. If you think about this, your friend will seem positively youthful. It is also possible that you disapprove of your friend's partner and feel they should not have been allowed to reproduce. Keep this to yourself.

Finally – many women can gain up to half a shoe size during pregnancy due to water retention. Do not mention this.

3. Try not to be smug

If you have had a baby yourself don't tell them what an easy time you had or how people who complain about morning sickness are just whingers. Every pregnancy and the physical impact it has on someone is unique.

4. Don't touch

Just because a woman is pregnant does not mean her body has become some kind of 'Open All Hours' zone for other people's hands. Touch her if she invites you to. It's also a good idea to talk directly to the woman and not, rather bizarrely, to start addressing your words to her belly.

Waiting for the baby

It's worth bearing in mind that in the nine months from conception to birth a baby's weight increases by 3,000 million times. That's a lot, and the last month is usually the most exhausting for a pregnant woman. Fewer than 10 per cent of babies are born on their exact due date, so this is not a good time to keep texting or ringing to see if the baby has arrived. Once she has been safely through labour, trust me, she will be telling everyone.

(If you count all the battles in Margaret Mitchell's epic novel, *Gone with the Wind*, then the character Melanie Hamilton is pregnant for twenty-one months. When someone pointed this out to the author she replied that a Southerner's pace is slower than that of a Yankee.)

Lesbian mothers

You would need to know a pregnant lesbian couple very well indeed before it was all right to ask, 'Where did you get the sperm?' or 'Did you have sex with the "father"?' How they got pregnant is private information and you need to let them tell you if they would like to.

THE ACTUAL BIRTH

*One has a strong wish to give a husband a good, strong ducking...
what humiliations to the delicate feelings of a poor woman,
especially with those nasty doctors. One really felt more like a cow or
a dog ...*

Queen Victoria on the subject of childbirth

Men used to be banned from the delivery room and people took the ban very seriously. In 1522 in Hamburg, a Dr Wertt was so keen to watch a woman in labour that he dressed up as a woman in order to get in. His ruse was discovered and he was burned at the stake. Later on, men were cut a bit more slack. My grandfather always associated the birth of his four children with going to buy loose tea. It was customary for babies to be born at home and when the moment for delivery was near, the midwife always sent my grandfather out to buy a packet of tea. She did not want him hanging around when the baby was born.

These days it is common for the father or partner to be present during birth but let's not for one moment imagine that this means he has much say in anything. There is no doubt that this is still a time when the woman gets to rule the roost. The expectant mother needs to be comfortable, so it is a good idea for everyone to be clear about what is wanted before the event. This is not a time for disputes. Some people like to turn the delivery room into a circus. There are even professional 'birth coaches'.

Make sure everyone has agreed to the level of excitement in the room beforehand. Booking a video director to turn up as a last-minute surprise may not go down well.

If you are not the one actually giving birth –

Do not interfere unless requested. No matter how devoted a potential grandmother might be, she needs to restrain herself at this time.

Gardening leave

I don't know whether to deal with this but it's the sort of topic that is widely discussed on pregnancy forums where I discovered the question – 'Is there an etiquette for the pruning of the lady garden during labour?!'

As far as I can ascertain there is no one answer. Many women, having put their bodies through nine months of strain, may not give a damn. It rather depends what you, or possibly your partner, are used to. If you are normally given to a Brazilian but have become rather 'overgrown' during the last nine months,

you may feel more comfortable having a tidy before a group of
strangers starts hanging out near your shrubbery waiting for the
baby to arrive.

(On the subject of the 'lady garden', there are many alternative
expressions for pubic hair of which my favourite is the Australian
hyponym, 'Map of Tasmania' also expressed, if you're in a terrible
hurry, as 'Mapatasi'.)

WELCOME LITTLE STRANGER

Everyone likes to share in good news and it would be a grumpy
soul who has no interest in the arrival of a family or friend's baby.
Throughout the centuries people have found ways of delivering
the good news. Sadly, the rather impressive 'star over the manger'
is not available to everyone. Any method of letting people know
is fine – proper newspaper notices, emails, phone calls, Facebook
status – although I'm not keen on anyone posting actual birth
videos. (It may just be me.)

The ancient Romans used to announce the arrival of a boy
by hanging an olive branch on the door of his parents' house
and a girl with a strip of woollen fabric. Early Americans would
sometimes embroider a pin cushion with the words 'Welcome
Little Stranger' and hang it on the front door, while in my native
Denmark it is still common for a family to put a picture of a stork
outside a newborn's home carrying a baby in either a pink or a
blue piece of cloth.

Send out messages about the good news as soon as possible,
remembering that people will want to know the basics – sex of
the child, weight, hair colour, that kind of thing. (Oddly no one is

ever interested in height.) These days many people do this by text or phone. It is often used as something to keep the father busy.

Birth announcement cards

These are less common because people haven't the energy but again should just contain the facts.

Receiving a birth announcement

You need to respond and you need to say something positive. If the child looks like a turnip do not say so. Also don't comment on the choice of name, however bizarre. The American actress Shannon Sossamon, who starred opposite Heath Ledger in the film *A Knight's Tale*, named her son 'Audio Science' which is, you know... different.

NEW PARENTHOOD

The mother

This a hard fact to get your head around when you are a new parent so I will be brutal – not everyone is as interested in the birth of your baby as you are. Shocking, isn't it? Some people are even squeamish about the details. There are also very few people, on the whole, who are interested in your child's bowel movements, no matter how focused you may become on them.

Don't be hurt if all the gifts coming into the house are for the baby and not for you. Now that you have a child you had better get used to coming second in life.

Be sensitive if one of your friends is having fertility treatment or has a history of miscarriage. Holding your baby may be too painful for them. Even if you are very tired don't tell them that they have had a lucky escape.

The father or parent not giving birth

I'm so sorry but honestly, no one is interested in you. Your time will come but this ain't it. Be supportive and help in ...

Dealing with visitors

Be very clear about how welcome people are and for how long. This is a good time to lay down boundaries, especially if there are competing sets of grandparents vying for time. Traditionally the maternal grandmother was allowed priority, but don't start a family feud. Sending a general text about when you, as new parents, will feel ready to receive visitors is a good way to head off too much attention. These days photos posted on a website can help stave off other people's curiosity. Again, consider how much others wish to see a close-up of a placenta.

Being a baby bore

I'm going to say it again because it will take a while to sink in – remarkable as your child may seem to you, it is probably no better or worse than any other child anywhere in the world. You have to accept that no one will ever have the strength of feeling that you have for your offspring. They may even (and this is shocking) find the child a pain. Here are some simple rules:

1. Don't keep boasting about your baby

It's just a baby. Everyone has been one.

2. No one wants to hear details about your milk production

Really. No one.

3. Don't keep mentioning your figure

If you get your figure back, well done. Everyone is delighted, but it is not a miracle. Don't go on about it. This is especially true with other new mums who have not been so fortunate and still look like something Drew Barrymore ought to save in a whaling movie.

4. Don't be smug about your baby's sleeping

The baby is not sleeping because you are a brilliant parent. You are just lucky to have one that likes to sleep. Parents with fractious children may want to kill you.

5. Accept change

Understand that your horizons have diminished into a world of sterilising things, changing nappies and being slightly demented with sleep loss. Know that this is not real and one day you will wake up.

FRIENDS AND FAMILY

When to visit

Shortly after the birth is fine as long as the new mother feels up to receiving visitors. Bring a gift for the child, flowers for the mother and a card for both. If the newborn has an older sibling already in place, know how seriously put out that child is going to be. A gift for them, too, is kind. When I was eleven my parents said they had a surprise for me. Turned out it was my sister. I thought we were getting a swimming pool. Disappointment doesn't really cover it.

Visiting new mothers at home

Having a new baby is exhausting. Don't turn up unexpectedly even if you used to drop in all the time. If you do visit, don't stay long, don't comment if the place is in chaos and do try to be helpful. If you want a cup of tea make it yourself. Think about the new timetable and don't phone for your usual late-night chat. Texting first to see how the land lies is a good idea.

Inviting new parents to an event

Don't be offended if they say no.

ADOPTION

People who have applied for a baby through adoption have been through a great deal. They have been investigated, had their lives, homes and finances checked in a way no one having a baby via sex can ever imagine. They have also generally waited longer for their child than any pregnancy. When the child arrives they deserve exactly the same fuss, gifts and offers of help as if the offspring, whatever age, shared their DNA.

BAPTISMS/CHRISTENINGS/NAMING CEREMONIES

These often have clear rules laid down by a particular faith. If you make your own ceremony you can, of course, decide on your own format. It is quite common for the parents at these ceremonies to select other adults to play a significant role in the child's life. In Christianity these are known as godparents.

The godparents used to be responsible for the child's religious education but these days even atheists are selected. Godparents are always selected by the parents. No one should volunteer. It is awkward if the family doesn't think you are suitable. If you are selected – be sure you are ready to commit to being in the child's life. It is possible to turn down being a godparent, but you are unlikely to stay friends with the couple.

Parents should be careful about their selection. When the French conductor and composer, Louis Antoine Jullien, was born in 1812, his father, a violinist, was working with the Sisteron Philharmonic Society orchestra in Alpes-de-Haute-Provence. He asked the orchestra to provide one of its thirty-six members to become the child's godfather. No one could agree, so the infant was named after all of them – Louis George Maurice Adolphe Roche Albert Abel Antonio Alexandre Noë Jean Lucien Daniel Eugène Joseph-le-brun Joseph-Barême Thomas Thomas Thomas-Thomas Pierre Arbon Pierre-Maurel Barthélemi Artus Alphonse Bertrand Dieudonné Emanuel Josué Vincent Luc Michel Jules-de-la-plane Jules-Bazin Julio César Jullien.

What to say at a Bris or Brit milah (Jewish circumcision)

Do say – '*Mazel tov*' to the parents and extended family. It means 'Good luck' in Yiddish.

Don't say – 'I bet that hurt.'

Random baby facts

A baby is born in the world every three seconds.

The protein that keeps a baby's skull from fusing is called 'noggin'.

Babies have no kneecaps. These don't develop for about six months. This is why you never see a baby kneeling.

Famous premature babies – Albert Einstein, Charles Darwin, Isaac Newton, Napoleon Bonaparte, Mark Twain, Pablo Picasso, Auguste Renoir, Stevie Wonder, Johann Goethe, and Sir Winston Churchill who was so unexpected he was born in a ladies' cloakroom. (There was a time when all new babies were said to look like Winston Churchill. Presumably he did, too.)

OUT AND ABOUT WITH BABY

Baby buggies

Buggies can be a bugger. The small, fold-up-like-an-umbrella ones are on the whole no trouble but some of the more expensive types, which appear to be designed to climb Everest while your child naps, can cause ructions. They take up a lot of space and some people don't view them kindly. Indeed in Canada, which otherwise seems such a peaceable place, there have been what are referred to as 'stroller wars'. In Halifax the police had to be called when six mothers and accompanying children in pushchairs had an hour-long stand-off with a bus driver who thought they were taking up too much space. It's that 'Consideration' issue. Let's all try to make room for each other. Don't clog up the aisle of anything unless you have to, don't run over anyone's feet with your mountain-climbing tyke trike and remember to park prettily.

Restaurants

It may be news to the new parent whose world has suddenly shrunk, but in a restaurant you are not the only person dining. The people around you may be there for all sorts of reasons – they may be having a romantic tryst, come from a funeral, be discussing business, etc. They do not want to hear your child wailing. Mouthing 'He's tired' will not make anyone feel better. If your baby cries, get up and take the child out of the room until it settles. It is not kind to ruin everyone's meal.

A newborn urinates about every twenty minutes. By the time they are six months old they are still weeing roughly every hour. They need about 7,500 nappy changes a year. This is a lot and it needs doing, but no diner wants to see your child's efforts while they are eating. If your child needs a fresh nappy, find somewhere private to sort it. Using the seat next to you is not appropriate.

BREASTFEEDING

This is an area that causes no end of trouble. Breastfeeding is good for a baby. I think we can all agree on that. What causes friction is where and how the breastfeeding takes place. The Equality Act 2010 states that you can't discriminate against a woman because she is breastfeeding. No one can stop you breastfeeding in public so a restaurant or café, for example, cannot refuse to serve you. However, what are the words we're looking for? Consideration and comfort.

The baby needs to be comfortable but it's not a bad idea if everyone else is, too. The fact is that the baby needs to get to your bare breast and not everyone may want to share the view.

In public

Be discreet. Of course your child's welfare is more important than other people's sensibilities, but it is perfectly possible to breastfeed a child without making it into a public display. The careful use of a shawl or muslin to cover yourself while the baby is latched on can mean a successful feed while not exposing yourself to strangers. If someone has a problem with you after that, keep calm and don't engage with their irritation. If you are being discreet no one should mind.

When someone else is breastfeeding in public

Don't stare.

Don't draw attention to it even if you don't like it.

Don't comment. If you must say something simply ask if it's a boy or a girl. Also ask yourself why you needed to say something.

BRINGING UP BABY

Evolutionary biologists posit that human beings are actually born too early. They appear at nine months not because they are fit to live outside the womb but because any further delay would mean that their heads would be too big to make their way through the birth canal. Cook a kid for longer than the recommended time and you would cause even more grief to the delivering mother than is the present case. It takes a human infant much longer to be able to look after itself than most baby animals, so they need self-love; they need to treat their primary carers as slaves supplying their every need. This period of parental servitude cannot, however, go on for ever so the question is …

When can you start teaching babies to behave?

The term 'infant' is from the Latin (yet again) *infans* which means 'unable to speak'. This period seems a bit of an unknown desert in our shaping because all of us have something called 'infantile amnesia' and can't recall much that happens to us before the age of three. This may be because memory is tied to language. Before kids can speak it is tough to teach them that they won't always come first.

Under six months

Babies have no capacity for being naughty. They also have a very short memory, so even if you try to indicate that something doesn't please you they won't remember. The best you can do is to be calm and know that they are not trying to annoy you. Getting angry because they cry just adds to the bedlam.

Under a year

Still that memory thing is not going all that well. Just because you told the baby yesterday not to touch the computer doesn't mean the computer isn't just as interesting today. The child may even touch it because your reaction is so very intriguing.

Good things to do

1. Be consistent

If the child is not allowed to touch the computer then have the same rule every day.

2. Begin gentle teaching

Use the word 'no' gently but firmly as you remove them from something they shouldn't be playing with. It will take ages for them to work out what you mean. Balance this by being clearly pleased with nice behaviour. Again, you're in for a long haul of repetition.

3. Distract them. Keep them safe

It is natural that they are curious about the world around them. Take them away from things which they shouldn't be playing with while explaining what you are doing. They may understand more than you think. I was once exasperated with my not-yet-speaking ten-month-old god-daughter's eating habits. There was food everywhere, including in her hair. 'You might as well tip the bowl over your head,' I said. So she did. This proves that a sense of sarcasm takes a while to develop.

Bad things to do

- Yelling
- Hitting

Both are pointless and confusing. There is no doubt enough noise in the house from the child without the parent joining in.

Be proportionate

Everyone wants kids to behave, not turn into an adult with social interaction issues. The movie director Alfred Hitchcock was by all accounts something of a prankster in his adulthood and not always a kind one. One of the theories about his sometimes unpleasant attitude to others is that the seeds were sown when he was five. His father William was a greengrocer and one day he sent young Alfred with a note to the local police chief. The chief locked the little boy in a cell for ten minutes before releasing him with the words 'That's what we do to naughty boys'. I expect that explains quite a lot.

Toddlers (age two to three)

The hardest job kids face today is learning good manners without seeing any.

Fred Astaire (1899–1987), dancer, actor and choreographer

There is a painting of a two-year-old boy by the sixteenth-century Dutch painter Jacob Willemszoon Delff called simply *Portrait of a Young Boy* in which the kid looks more like a miniature adult than a toddler. There are those who reckon 'childhood' is a relatively modern concept. Certainly during the early years of the Industrial Revolution children as young as four worked in factories, and the Victorians famously had no problem shoving kids up chimneys or down mine shafts.

It is the eighteenth-century philosopher Jean-Jacques Rousseau who is often credited with being the first to see childhood as a series of developmental phases. He believed that a child up to the age of twelve was guided merely by emotion, but after that age and over the next four years, reason starts to take hold, while from sixteen and upwards the adult begins to form. Certainly by my third child of three I realised that there was a very simple benchmark for working out when your offspring is capable of genuinely good behaviour. It's when they finally have the motor skills to colour in properly. While they still scribble wildly with crayons, parenting is the most tiresomely repetitive time and the grown-ups just need to take a deep sigh and get used to it.

Toddler time is about endlessly reminding youngsters that they need to think about others. They can begin to be taught the basics about:

- Sharing
- Gentleness

● Please and thank you

Say it yourself and say it often, until it becomes so boring you could scream.

Do not scream.

Playgroup Manners for Parents

1. Make your child be the nice one

If your child keeps snatching toys from others or bashing them on the head or biting – stop them! If you don't, you won't make friends with the other parents who then won't invite you back for a drink. You may well need a drink.

2. Keep infection in the family

If your child is sick then stay home, no matter how desperate you are to see another adult. Some people do have 'pox parties' or 'flu flings' to infect kids deliberately in order to boost their immunity. Personally I think this is on the suspect side. There have even been cases in the US of parents passing a whistle from an infected child to other kids. This is bonkers. Who wants a sick child with a whistle?

3. Stay in charge

Most playgroups are not a babysitting service. You still need to be in charge of your kid.

4. Be helpful

No one enjoys putting away toys. Do your share.

5. Be nice

No matter how much you loathe someone's child, remember its parents adore the little monster. Keep your views to yourself. If a child is naughty but is not yours, refer the incident to the mother or person in charge. Then go home and be glad the kid is not coming with you.

GROWING UP

Still he wallowed and rolled up and down himself in the mire and dirt – he blurred and sullied his nose with filth – he blotted and smutched his face with any kind of scurvy stuff – he trod down his shoes in the heel – at the flies he did oftentimes yawn, and ran very heartily after the butterflies, the empire whereof belonged to his father. He pissed in his shoes, shit in his shirt, and wiped his nose on his sleeve – he did let his snot and snivel fall in his pottage, and dabbled, paddled, and slobbered everywhere – he would drink in his slipper, and ordinarily rub his belly against a pannier.

François Rabelais, *Gargantua and Pantagruel*, Volume I, c. 1532

Gargantua was a giant who had the bad manners to kill his mother during childbirth. With such a poor start he went on to become a nightmare youth. Many manners books over the years have been directed at children and indeed many rules exist simply to avoid the sometimes, let's be frank, disgusting behaviour of the fledgling human. Having your own kids means getting over any number of taboos about dealing, for example, with another person's excreta. The most important thing to recall is that no one has the same strength of feeling towards a child that a parent has. If you want your child to be popular, you need to help them learn how to get along with the rest of the world.

Saying hello

Teach your kid to look people in the eye when they meet someone new. Show them how much nicer it is if they smile and give their name clearly. Lydgate wrote,

> Who-so speke to þee in ony maner place,
> lumpischli caste not þin heed a-doun,
> but with a sad cheer loke him in þe face.

Basically, when spoken to, don't lumpishly look at the ground but look someone cheerfully in the face. It's still a good plan. In the UK if a person asks 'How are you?' it's a good idea to teach children that the correct response is 'Fine, thank you'. No British person actually wants a detailed answer to the enquiry. The next stage is to get the child to be interested in anyone but themselves and enquire 'How are you?' back.

Don't let them be sullen

It's a splendid word 'sullen'. It originally just meant 'solitary' but now it merely stands for rudeness. Children who don't answer when addressed by someone else need to understand that this is not a good way for us all to get along. They are the kids who don't get invited to someone else's house for tea. They are also the ones the teachers don't pick for special treats.

Early school years (age four to eleven years)

I think you can tell a lot about what kind of an adult you are going to get by the behaviour of a child. George W. Bush, who went on to become the forty-third president of the United States, is an interesting example. According to his childhood friend, Terry Throckmorton, he and George spent their summers in Midland, Texas, putting firecrackers in frogs and throwing them so that they would blow up. It is tempting to wonder if perhaps George's parents had had a word it might have saved the world a lot of trouble later on.

While you are still a kid it is no doubt hard to imagine that one day you may spend a lot of money on therapists trying to untangle what your parents did to you. As the old saying goes, 'A Freudian slip is like saying one thing, but meaning your mother.' This is the age when the concept of 'His Majesty the Baby' really ought to be being put away. Now the child starts to have an early social life at both school and play and some of it will be without the parents. Children need to know how to survive in social inter-action, so there are some essential early lessons. Many of them were covered in *Stans Puer ad Mensam – The Book of Curteisie*, a book of children's manners ascribed to John Lydgate in 1430. The basics haven't really changed in 600 years and it really comes down to the three Rs of interaction.

Respect for Self
Respect for Others
Responsibility

At school

Ideally school is the place where children are taught to think. Choosing the right kind of education for your child can be a nightmare for any parent. It was something the poet Percy Bysshe Shelley never had to consider for his son Percy. Shelley had always been something of a maverick. By the age of nineteen he had been expelled from Oxford and eloped with a sixteen year old. When he died his son, Percy Florence, whom he had had with his second wife, Mary Shelley, was only three. Mary was recommended to send Percy to a particular school at which he would be 'taught to think for himself'. 'To think for himself!' she is said to have replied in horror. 'Oh, my God, teach him to think like other people!'

If you think about the difficulties you may have with one child, try multiplying that into a playground full. The school will have rules for a reason. Teach your kid to stick to them. Years ago I asked one of my kids what she thought was a good rule to learn for school when you start. She said, 'Don't poo your pants in the playground.' Apparently a child had done this in Year 1 and it was still the talk of the place in Year 3.

School Rules

These rules echo so much of what we've already looked at. They are in short form exactly the same guidelines for almost any social occasion later in life with a group of people.

1. Turn up on time.

2. Have the right kit.

3. Pay attention.

4. Don't answer back.

5. Try to get along with everyone.

6. Don't steal, cheat, lie or any of the other basics.
7. Don't poo your pants in the playground (I nearly forgot that one).

FIRST SOCIAL EVENTS

Birthday parties

The Egyptians ... discovered to which of the gods each month and day is sacred; and found out from the day of a man's birth, what he will meet with in the course of his life, and how he will end his days, and what sort of man he will be.

Herodotus, *Persian Wars*, Book II

There is only one birthday in the Bible and it's for a pharaoh (Genesis 40: 20–22). It can't have gone all that well because at the end of the festivities the Egyptian leader 'hanged the chief baker'. I've had cakes I wasn't keen on but that seems a little extreme. Traditionally neither Christians nor Jews marked the day. Not even the birth of Jesus seems to have been an excuse for a party. The first-century historian Josephus said Jewish law forbade such celebrations because they afforded 'occasion of drinking to excess'. There is some comfort in knowing how little human behaviour has changed over the years. The Jews were of course right. Even the genius Shakespeare failed to show restraint, dying on his birthday in 1616. According to a Stratford clergyman called John Ward, 'Shakespear, Drayton, and Ben Jonson had a merry meeting, and it seems drank too hard, for Shakespear died of a fever there contracted.'

The history of birthdays

You might think that because everyone who was ever born had a birthday then the concept has no history, but the marking of birthdays probably has a pagan origin. Birthdays used to be seen as a fearful experience. Personal spirits were said to be particularly keen to hang around on the day you were born and this apparently made you susceptible to spells both good and evil. Any dreams during the night before needed remembering as they might predict the future. With all this nonsense going on it was a good idea to protect yourself by gathering together as many well-wishers as possible.

Gifts are a reminder of sacrifices offered to pagan gods on their birthdays and the cake with candles relates to pagan notions about the magic of fire. The Greeks used to celebrate the birthday of Artemis, the moon goddess, by putting candles on a cake to make it seem like her home turf, the moon. They believed the smoke from the candles carried their prayers to the goddess. We echo this when we make a wish and blow out the candles.

GIVING A BIRTHDAY PARTY

The parents

1. Make the numbers manageable

A good guide is to invite the same number of children as your child's age plus one. Don't risk having more kids than you can cope with. It's very bad manners to return children in a worse state than you received them.

2. The invitation

You can send these by email but it suggests you didn't take the time to plan properly. Getting the kids to help write their own invitations is part of the fun. Most parents are busy and exhausted.

They want a piece of paper they can stick on the fridge with all the necessary information.

3. Length of party
Don't exhaust other people's children. You will regret it. Their parents will hate you.

Up to age 3: one hour
4–7: an hour and a half
8–12: two hours
12+: good luck getting it over with

4. Other parents
This party is for the kids. It is not your chance to trump the party some other parent gave for their child. There is no need to pick an outlandish location for the party just because someone else did. Find out what your kid wants. If you want a parent to stay with their child, say so on the invitation. For kids under the age of five expect parents to stay anyway.

5. Addressing the envelopes
Address the invitation to the person being invited. If you want Lord Fauntleroy to come alone put 'Lord Fauntleroy' on the envelope. If you want him to bring his family put 'Lord Fauntleroy and Family'. If you don't want Lord Fauntleroy there at all, do try to remember it's your kid's guest list, not yours.

6. Chasing RSVPs
Phone and check if someone hasn't replied. You will need to know numbers.

7. Deal calmly and quickly with bad behaviour
There is nothing more likely to trigger tantrums or crazy behaviour than too much sugar, some E numbers and a few party games. Keep calm and try to direct the children's energies elsewhere. Get them to help you with something. If there is a

particular troublemaker, remove them from the group and let them settle down a little before rejoining. Never shout at other people's kids, however tempted you might be.

8. Don't get cross with the birthday child

Again – however tempted you might be. Don't ruin their day just because they may not have coped brilliantly. Maybe suggest a quick game of 'Sleeping Lions' and see who can be the sleepiest King of the Jungle on the floor.

9. Make a list of who came and who gave what

You will need it for thank-you notes.

10. Send thank-you notes

The Children

Birthday cakes should always have pink icing on the top, with the name of the birthday boy or girl spelt out in preserved cherries.

Manners for Women by Mrs Humphry (Madge of Truth), 1898

Explain what you expect to your kid before the party. You can even practise these things before the event. Depending on the age, the expected behaviour should eventually include:

1. Saying hello to everyone who arrives.
2. Looking after guests first.
3. Being equally nice to everyone.
4. Not expecting to win all the games.
5. Not forgetting all table manners.
6. Thanking each person for coming.
7. Opening the presents after everyone has gone. It saves time, avoids the awkwardness of the honest reaction to an unwanted gift and may avert jealousy from the guests. Teach your child to be grateful for every present even the awful ones and to write a thank-you note. We used to allow our kids to

invite their entire class to a party, but it was on condition that everyone who came received a thank-you note afterwards even if it was just a scribble to begin with.

8. Thank your own parents for their heroic efforts.

ATTENDING A BIRTHDAY PARTY

The parents of an invitee

1. Offer to help out

If your child is small you will be expected to stay at the party and not go home to sleep, which might be your preferred option. If your child is not so small it is still polite to offer.

2. Don't dump your other kids at the party

If you have no one to look after your other children, ask the host if you can leave your child by itself. Then it is up to the host to suggest you bring more kids.

Going too far

A birthday should celebrate the simple fact that someone is alive. There is no need to go overboard. When the defence contractor David Brooks spent $10 million on his daughter's thirteenth birthday party he was definitely going too far. (This may have been a theme with him as he later went too far in business and was charged with embezzlement.) The hotel heiress Paris Hilton celebrated her twenty-first birthday with six parties in five time zones, spending an alleged £45,000 per guest, while the Sultan of Brunei marked his own fiftieth with a party said to have cost $27.2 million. You don't need all that. There is nothing cheerier than a few balloons, too much jelly and games with parcels. Even in my mature years I can be made entirely happy by pinning the tail of a donkey in an entirely inappropriate place.

PETS

Animals are such agreeable friends – they ask no questions; they pass no criticisms.

George Eliot (1819–80), author

Some people have pets as well as children. Some have them instead of children. Please notice that I haven't called this section '*Owning Pets*' and that is because it is rare that anyone seems in full charge of a domesticated animal. If you think the baby grabs the title 'His Majesty' then that is nothing compared to the number of pets who vie to be the emperor. There are, of course, plenty of responsible people with pets. They already know how to behave. For the rest I'll try to take it slowly.

The basics

It's a bit like children. In fact, it's a lot like children but without the many years of colouring in (unless your pet is particularly advanced). Often the pet in your life has not only entered your home but your heart as well. You love them in a way that people who don't have pets find a little odd or even creepy. It seems astonishing to you that everyone doesn't feel the same about Fido or Tiddles as you do, so here is a really bald fact –

They don't.

There are even people who don't like animals at all.

Very nice people.

So, basic manners – we all need to rub along and think about each other. This includes domesticated animals. If the animals can't manage to co-exist with the rest of society then they are less domesticated than anyone might have hoped.

DOGS

Outside of a dog, a book is a man's best friend. Inside of a dog it's too dark to read.

Groucho Marx, American comedian, 1890–1977

We don't know exactly how long man has been trying to turn the dog into his best friend. Fifteen thousand years perhaps, or maybe less or maybe more. Honestly, we have no idea. A long time. The close relationship began because both dog and human got something out of it. The dog got regular food and the human felt protected. Looking at the current services available for dogs it may be that the animals are doing better than before. There are about ten and a half million dogs in the UK and their humans can purchase a water bowl for them shaped like a toilet, seek canine acupuncture and therapy and it probably won't be long before 'Doga', you guessed it, yoga for dogs, makes its way across the Atlantic from New York.

Dogs are much loved and this is splendid as long as everyone works out how to co-exist.

For the person with a pet dog

1. Do make sure you have time for a dog

I'm going to assume that if you get a dog you will love it. It's cute, right? It loves you back no matter how vile you are. So, if you love your dog then you need to find time for it. If you leave a dog alone for too long the chances are it will become distressed and start barking. It's not fair to the dog or anyone else. The neglected animal is going to be a nightmare when you finally take it out in public.

2. Do keep your dog quiet in public places

Public spaces are by their very nature there to be shared. They are not simply a place provided for your animal's entertainment. People may be trying to chat, to enjoy the sound of the birds or they may even live nearby and are trying to sleep or work. All dogs can be trained not to bark. If they bark unnecessarily it is because you haven't taken the time to teach them how irritating it is.

3. Pick up dog mess

It's that pesky public space thing again. There are very few areas devoted entirely to providing canine toilet facilities. If you wish to convert your own garden into a pooch poo palace, help yourself. If your dog is – how can I put this? – a messy reliever, make sure you clean the affected fur. If you don't, the dog is bound to sit down on someone else's carpet and leave a souvenir.

4. Teach your dog to sit or walk to heel

You might save its life if you can stop it running into the road. You might also prevent an accident. Show some respect for road users who don't want to injure your animal and will feel terrible if they do. Ideally, keep the dog on a leash when you are out so that you have full control. Don't let your dog jump up at anyone. Even people you know well may be wearing nice clothes.

5. Don't let your dog run around where people are eating

People sitting in a pub garden on a restaurant terrace may not want your dog slobbering at their crotch.

6. Don't let your dog slobber at someone's crotch

I don't need to explain that, right?

7. Don't bring your dog with you to someone's home without asking

If you have been invited to dinner that invitation doesn't usually include the dog. Don't presume people won't mind if you turn up with the pooch. If you do visit, do not allow the dog on the furniture even if you think it does no harm. I had a friend visit with two large dogs. I very clearly asked if she would mind not letting them sit on the sofa. When they jumped up on to my new settee she just shrugged and said, 'What can you do?' Well, you can not come again, that's for sure.

8. If someone says to you that they are frightened of dogs – believe them

They are not trying to annoy you and one solitary encounter with your canine is unlikely to fix the problem. It's worth bearing in mind that the domestic dog is a subspecies of the grey wolf and some people don't see a lot of difference. It's the same with allergies. Don't try to test your particular breed against the skin of someone who says they are allergic. Even if you think it's nonsense you don't want to be the one left hunting for an all-night chemist.

CATS

When my cats aren't happy, I'm not happy. Not because I care about their mood but because I know they're just sitting there thinking up ways to get even.

Attributed to Percy Bysshe Shelley (1792–1822), English poet
(although it seems most unlikely)

There is lovely story about President Calvin Coolidge. At breakfast one morning, a guest at the White House watched with astonishment as he quietly poured some milk from his cup into a saucer. Fearful of committing some unforeseen breach of etiquette, the guest followed suit. Then, without a word, Coolidge bent down and placed the saucer on the floor for the cat, which had been waiting unobserved beneath the table.

There are almost as many cats in the UK as dogs, and again the possibilities for spoiling them are endless. You can buy feline playhouses shaped like a tank, a plane or a fire engine and there's even a boutique luxury hotel group just for moggies. I can only presume the mini-bar is packed with catnip.

Most of the rules about dogs apply to cats except possibly the one about barking. I am fifty-five years old and I am frightened of cats. It makes no sense and I have tried to conquer it, but the fear remains. I can't tell you how many times people have assured me 'My cat is the softest thing. She won't hurt you.' They have left the room and their unsupervised tabby has taken a lump out of my leg. I doubt things will change in my lifetime.

In addition:

Clean your cat's litter box
You become desensitised to smells in your own home. You may even grow used to the smell of used cat litter. Visitors' noses haven't had that opportunity.

Hoover up cat hair
Nobody wants it on their clothing. Nobody. These are hairs even the cat didn't want.

KEEPING A NON-DOMESTIC PET

I like pigs. Dogs look up to us. Cats look down on us. Pigs treat us as equals.

Sir Winston Churchill (1874–1965), British politician

There is a really simple rule of thumb – if the animal you are thinking of bringing into your life requires the word 'enclosure' in order to look after it then you might want to think again. The very term 'non-domestic pet' suggests a creature that struggles to be house-trained.

1. Can you really look after it?
Are you being mean to the animal by keeping it in a small flat when what it really needs is a few acres of savannah? The animal deserves your consideration. Are you sure you know a vet who can deal with any potential illnesses?

2. What will your neighbours think?
Unless you live in the middle of nowhere entirely by yourself you need to consider the impact of an unusual animal taking up residence in your neighbourhood. When I was a child in the US

it was common place for New Yorkers to return from holidays in Florida with a foot-long, live baby alligator. Urban legend had it that when these creatures grew too big the owners flushed them down the toilet and that the Manhattan sewage system was awash with alligators. I spent my youth in trepidation of being attacked from behind while being excused.

If you do have kids, Mary, try and recall that childhood ought to be a time of wonder. Gift that to your offspring along with a sense that they also need to co-exist with others at the same time. We all ought to have room to marvel at the world and manners help give us the necessary space.

Let's see, where we've got to? We've covered love and marriage and offspring (or other creatures you might be in charge of) and all the things that mean happily ever after when things go well. But, sadly, it's not always like that and there are times when even the nicest person can feel like blowing up a few frogs. I hate to have to mention it but we probably should take a quick look at what to do when things go wrong.

Much love

Sandi

10: BREAKING UP IS HARD TO DO

Dear Mary

Oh dear, this is a sad bit. I've kept it brief as I hope you will never need it. Ideally one should work on a relationship which is proving problematic. If the partnership is just a little stale, then the best thing is to see if something can be done to perk things up. Having said that, it is, of course, better to depart from failure with dignity than to stay and build further recriminations. This chapter is about all sorts of breaking up – marriage, friendship, business partnerships and so on. You may be the breaker or the breakee (no such word, I know but it covers the gist); either way it can all be painful and all needs managing. Sadly, you are bound to encounter matters from both sides, but let's start with the times when you decide something is over. The first things to remember are:

1. Don't be in a rush

You could just be irritated. Also bear in mind that after a relationship breakup comes dating again and that can be just an awful lot of effort. You will have to start holding your stomach in again and everything.

2. Consider your own part in the breakup

It's probably not all one person's fault. While you may want to tar your partner or friend with the bastard brush, consider the remote possibility that you may have used the same brush yourself.

Once you are sure this is what you want to do, consider how to tell the person you are breaking up with.

Telling the other person

1. Where possible do it in person

Ideally, this is not something to do electronically. It's best to face the person, if only to remind yourself why you want to get away. There are exceptions. If the person has to travel a long way just to be told it is over then using the phone would be kinder. Kindness is the key. Try and imagine it is you who is being left and how you would feel. Coming back to a shared home to find the house stripped of your loved one's possessions with a Post-it note on the fridge saying they've left is not the nicest way to find out. Be brave. I had a friend who moved house rather than tell her partner she wanted out. It was a very expensive and rather startling way of breaking up.

2. Allow a dignified exit

Let your former partner leave with dignity. If the breakup is a shock, then perhaps telling them in a public place like a restaurant is not going to be the most thoughtful location.

3. Timing

Try to be nice about the time and place for the breakup. If you do it on Christmas Day or their birthday then that's probably not a great parting gift. Linking the breakup with a day that can't be forgotten is never kind.

4. Be calm and clear

Shouting at this stage is not helpful. Be aware that the person you are breaking up with may think everything is fine. Even if this astonishing lack of realisation about your feelings is part of why you are leaving, try to be calm.

5. Be kind

Try to remember something positive about the start of your relationship. The other person may be devastated. This is one time when it is all right to lie as you search for something positive about the past. This is a fine balancing act as it mustn't be so positive that they can't understand why you are off. If you really want to leave then make sure you don't leave the possibility of a reunion on the cards.

Receiving the news

Oh Mary, if I could make it true by wishing, then you would only ever have relationships with nice people. In theory when someone leaves you, the same things ought to apply as when you leave them. Although it can be hard to feel generous towards someone who is pushing off if you don't want them to, try to remember to be positive about the past, etc. It is not always possible at first glance to spot the brute who's disguised in a nice suit, and regrettably you may find yourself breaking up with someone who is not kind. It may happen that someone will break up with you who doesn't have the decency to do it well. If you need time to think, say so. Don't be bullied into anything. If you leave with nothing else from the relationship then try to keep your dignity.

Discuss:

Whether you are going to have any future contact.

What to do about mutual friends / his or her family with whom you may have become close.

Revenge

An eye for an eye will only make the whole world blind.

Mahatma Gandhi (1869–1948), Indian leader

It's never a very good idea, but you wouldn't be human if you weren't tempted. If you absolutely must have revenge then do at least try to be creative. Consider the woman who got back at her philandering husband by distributing his much-prized wine collection to her neighbours by placing one bottle alongside their milk delivery. He was devastated, she got a very dignified revenge and the neighbours are still talking about it. If you can't be that ingenious then maybe it's best just to move on.

If you live together and you are doing the leaving

1. Make a plan

Don't suddenly leave your former lover or friend homeless. They will only end up on a mutual friend's couch and soon someone else will resent you too. Try not to be in too much of a hurry. Give your former partner time to work out what to tell people. Move slowly toward an agreement about which one of you is going to move out and when. Don't presume you get to keep the home. If you are the one leaving the relationship you may find you are also the one leaving the home.

2. Don't be mean

Don't sweat the small stuff. You are starting afresh and who knows, you might even grow to like a new doormat.

If you live together and you are being left

1. Try and be practical

This is very hard if your heart is broken, so perhaps get a friend to help. Just because you are in pain does not mean your former partner can walk all over you. Make sure the breaking up of the home is equitable and fair.

2. Stop fighting

It's over. Spending more time trying to apportion blame is not going to help. You won't agree anyway. Besides, there is nothing more irritating than someone you want to fight with (or who wants to fight with you) refusing to engage.

Both of you

1. Don't tell everyone everything

There are several reasons for this including:

- If you bad-mouth your ex they will feel free to do the same to you.

- There is still a remote possibility that you might get back together. How will you feel if your friends now have all the dirt?

2. Take a breath

If it has been a long-term relationship take your time before taking up with someone else or you are bound to bore the new person.

3. Look forward

One of the exasperating things about pets or children (I have quite a list) is that they sometimes bind you to someone you can't stand the sight of. You need to sort this out. Ideally write down your plan as it is amazing how two people can have such different memories of the same agreement. Look what happened with Hitler and Chamberlain.

DIVORCE

Why write? Why struggle? You will do no good! but if everyone lacked courage with that doubt, nothing would ever be achieved in this world.

Caroline Norton (1808–77), British social reformer
agitating for divorce

I've never divorced but that may be only because up until fairly recently I wasn't allowed to get married. I shan't go through the minutiae as I'm sure you don't need me to tell you why you should leave someone – they are unkind, your overriding feeling for them is pity, you've found someone else, or it's simply that they like to spend weekends dusting the coat hangers and you've had enough. Because humans are human and sometimes don't get along, divorce litters history. You find it among the Egyptians and the Greeks. The Romans were rather keen divorcers and even the *Code of Hammurabi* in ancient Babylonia laid down rules for separating married couples legally. It was probably no easier an emotional ride then than now.

In medieval times only the church could grant a divorce. The slightly draconian rules eased a bit in the eighteenth and early nineteenth century when warring couples needed an Act of Parliament to legally leave each other. This meant a lot of poor people had to stay together. Thanks to Caroline Norton (well worth reading about) *The Matrimonial Causes Act 1857* was passed, which introduced divorce through the court. Today, about 42 per cent of UK marriages end with a formal dissolution and at the time of writing, the current starting price for a fast divorce online is £97. I'm not entirely sure how it works, but it's surely not as stressful and considerably less expensive than that entire Reformation that Henry VIII had to go through to divorce Catherine of Aragon. (Henry's petition to the Vatican to divorce Catherine is the weightiest one in history. The actual paperwork weighed 2.5 kilos and had eighty-one wax seals hanging off it like a beaded curtain. You can buy a replica for £43,000 if you fancy.)

Most expensive divorces (estimates)

Rupert Murdoch's divorce from Anna Murdoch – £1 billion

Bernie Ecclestone's divorce from Slavica – £760 million

Adnan Khashoggi's divorce from Soraya Khashoggi – £540 million

Paul McCartney's divorce from Heather Mills – £25 million

That's quite a lot of money. If you decide that you want a divorce then be certain that you really want out and not just a short break. Getting divorced is as big a step as getting married. Don't have one of those on–off marriages because it's maddening for others.

Both parties in a divorce

1. Be discreet

If you have terrible things to say about your partner, say them to a close friend or even a therapist. You never know how these things will come back to trouble you.

2. Consider family and friends

We all invest something in the relationships of those closest to us. Understand that your nearest and dearest may be upset, too.

3. Mind the kids if there are any

No matter how unhappy a marriage, most kids don't want their parents to divorce. If you have kids don't use them as pawns to get back at your ex. You may be breaking up with your partner but they are still a parent to your children who may be devastated by the split. Don't tell your kids details that they don't need to know.

People get divorced for all sorts of reasons

He taught me housekeeping; when I divorce I keep the house.

Zsa Zsa Gabor, actress b. 1917, seven divorces, one annulment

1. Because of a bird

In 2001 a woman in China divorced her husband when their pet mynah bird began repeating the phrases, 'I love you', 'be patient' and 'divorce' which it had overheard from the man's secret phone calls to his lover. Evidence from the bird was not permitted in court. (*Xinmin Evening News*)

2. Because of cleanliness

In 2009 a German woman divorced her husband, Christian Kropp of Sondershausen, after fifteen years of marriage because he kept cleaning. The last straw was when he knocked down a wall and rebuilt it because he couldn't get it as clean as he wanted.

3. Because of the mother-in-law

In 2005 a Romanian woman divorced her husband because she couldn't stand having lunch with her mother-in-law every day.

4. Because of a broken penis extension

Grigory Toporov of Voronezh, southern Russia, had a penis extension fitted to please his wife. Unfortunately it broke off in, um, 'mid flight' and she sued for divorce.

5. Because of the world's biggest lie

This is an apocryphal story which did the rounds on the internet after 9/11, but it says something about being caught out. It alleged that a man who worked on the 103rd floor of the World Trade Center spent the morning of 11 September at his mistress's flat with his phone and the television off. When he put the phone back on his wife rang. She was hysterical. 'Are you OK?' she demanded. 'Where are you?' He couldn't understand her anxiety. 'What do you mean? I'm in my office, of course.'

Dealing with your own ex

1. Be nice

When I was a kid in the US there were paper cups in dispensers called 'Dixie cups'. These came in many colours and were a feature in bathrooms and kitchens. You used a cup and threw it away. These days this would be seen as environmentally unfriendly. Equally, having a 'Dixie cup' mentality towards people is a bad idea. There must have been something about your ex that you liked in the first place. Think. Come on, really think. Anything? They left you? OK, that does make it tougher.

2. Let them know you've moved on

Don't let your ex find out you are dating again by reading it on Facebook or Twitter or hearing about it through the grapevine.

'Nice'

Everyone over-uses the odd word (I'm quite bored with politicians wearing out the term 'robust'.) I realise I use the word 'nice' quite a lot which is, well, odd because it's actually not a very 'nice' word. Don't worry; it's not Latin. It comes from twelfth-century French meaning 'careless, clumsy; weak; poor, needy; simple, stupid, silly, foolish'. From these less than attractive origins the word has had quite a journey. It began as 'foolish', two hundred years later became 'fussy', a hundred years on 'precise or careful' and finally some 600 years from the start (1830 if you must know) the term had been transformed into a way to claim something as kind and thoughtful. Nice.

3. Don't go out with their family

Brothers, sisters, mothers, fathers – all off limits unless you really really want to appear on the Jeremy Kyle Show.

4. Consider your new relationship

Being too cosy with your ex can make your current beau very anxious. Consider this if you all meet up. There is no reason to get rid of all photographic evidence of your past life but perhaps don't have it out on the mantelpiece.

5. Don't compare your new love to your ex

Saying what a great cook your ex was when the dinner is burning is never going to go well. According to the Roman historian Suetonius (c. 69–122), Tiberius, the stepson of the emperor Augustus, was forced to divorce his wife Vispania in 11 BC because she had failed to produce an heir. Tiberius then married Julia the Elder but one day he ran into Vispania and followed her home crying, begging her for forgiveness. Augustus had to arrange for them never to meet again. This was, of course, easier in the age before Facebook.

Dealing with your partner's ex

1. Discuss it

Talk to your partner, if you can, and his or her family about the relationship with the ex. Try to set some boundaries.

2. Don't let others tell you what to do

Some couples manage the relationship with their exes very well indeed. Don't let other people tell you how the dynamic ought to function.

3. Be nice

There it is again, but it is honestly easier. If they don't want to be nice back then at least you have the moral high ground.

4. Get used to it

Some relationships come with more baggage than others, especially if that baggage comes shaped like a child. Try to be relaxed. If someone was married for a very long time to the mother or father of their kids then they will always be in some kind of family relationship with each other. They may even remain in a relationship with other extended members of the ex's family. (My ex and my present partner get on very well which is good, except that I know they talk about me which is less good.)

Don't keep blaming your partner for having had a past. The fact is, kids come first. Never try to turn a child against either of its parents. If you say bad things about your partner's ex to the kids it will get reported back and cause trouble.

Dealing with a couple who are breaking up

1. Don't take sides

Honestly, you don't want to get involved. You'll find yourself on the phone at all hours to someone not thinking clearly.

2. Be available

OK, not too available as it can get a bit repetitive, but do try for the 'sympathetic without being partisan' approach.

3. Don't gossip

Don't even repeat the thing about the penis extension failure, no matter how tempting.

4. Be careful

Personally, if both parties were due to attend an event I was hosting, I'd rather call it off and descale the kettle. Instead you could speak to them both about the best way forward.

5. Rehabilitate

When the divorce is done, find time to party (although maybe don't invite the kids who will be less ready to celebrate.)

Hunnish practices

Having said not to gossip, there remain some high profile divorce cases which even years later keep tongues wagging. When John 'Stilts' Russell (who was by all accounts both heir to Lord Ampthill and a transvestite), married Christabel Hart in 1918 she refused to have sex with him because she didn't care for it. Nevertheless in 1921 she produced a son called Geoffrey. Stilts said he couldn't possibly be the father and sued for divorce on the grounds of the marriage never having been consummated. Christabel claimed that the baby arrived due to her husband's 'Hunnish practices'. The case went to court and the press had a ball. Christabel won her case, set up a very successful shop in Mayfair and the reporting of the best bits of divorce cases was banned, with no one any clearer what 'Hunnish practices' might be. (To save you looking it up, Mary, let me assure you that not even the Internet throws any light, either.)

CIVIL PARTNERSHIPS

Civil partnerships are dissolved, which makes them sound like a hangover cure. It's roughly the same as divorce except that it can't be applied for on the basis of adultery. I'm not sure why. I think the House of Lords couldn't bear to discuss the exact physical requirements for that to take place. Anyway, I know you're an empathic person so you will know instinctively that the pain and distress is exactly the same as divorce.

I expect you will break up with someone at some time. It's part of the process of working out what you want and need in life. The brilliant writer Margaret Atwood once said 'a divorce is like an amputation: you survive it, but there's less of you.' I love being married. I hope you find someone splendid like I did to be your life partner.

Much love

Sandi

11: BUYING THE FARM

I think I've discovered the secret of life – you just hang around until you get used to it.

Sally, Charlie Brown's sister, *Peanuts* (Charles Schulz, 1922–2000)

Dear Mary

I'm heading to the end of the life cycle (in this volume. Hopefully not in actuality because I have debts to repay ...) so we need to talk about the one thing every human being has in common – we are all going to die sometime. When I was a kid in the United States it wasn't uncommon for someone's passing to be announced by the expression 'He bought the farm'. As far as I know, the expression came from the rural community when a farm owner with life insurance would finally, upon dying, be able to buy his own property. This rather suggests that others may be better off if you die and is possibly on the materialistic side.

No matter what kinds of lives we lead – fame or anonymity, wealth or poverty – all our lives are bookended in exactly the same way: we must be born and we will inevitably die. About 10,000 people an hour die in the world, so even before our own demise it is something we will have to face at some point. Consider Saladin, the Sultan of Egypt who in the twelfth century had managed to conquer Syria, Arabia, Persia, Mesopotamia, and taken Jerusalem.

When he died in 1193 he left instructions that the shirt he was wearing at death be carried on the end of a spear through the camp, with a soldier proclaiming

> Behold all that remains of the Emperor Saladin. Of all the states he had conquered, of all the provinces he had subdued, of the boundless treasures he had amassed, of the countless wealth he possessed, he retained in dying nothing but this shroud.

I rather like Saladin. He entirely hedged his bets on religion, leaving money to Muslim, Jewish and Christian leaders to intercede on his behalf to God. Anyway, I'm avoiding dealing with the topic at hand. We must crack on to the end and look at how to behave well in the face of grief.

DEALING WITH DEATH

Dying is a very dull, dreary affair. And my advice to you is to have nothing whatever to do with it.

W. Somerset Maugham (1874–1965), English dramatist and novelist

Speaking to the bereaved

1. Check if there are any specific customs you should know about

Orthodox Jews, for example, believe that the body should be shrouded and buried on the day of death, while Buddhists believe that consciousness stays in the body for three days. Check that you know what the bereaved believe.

2. Seeing the bereaved

How soon you do this depends on how close you are. If it is immediate family you should visit a bereaved person as soon as possible. If you can't go in person then telephone. This is a moment for one-to-one communication. If the news is emailed to you or even texted, it is fine to reply in kind, but check to see if a follow-up visit would be welcome. A handwritten letter or card is always appreciated. The bereaved may not be up to much chatting on the phone.

3. Don't talk about yourself
No one cares if you are getting divorced, have lost your job, your keys, your health, etc. However bad things are you are not dead. This is not your moment.

4. Say something
It is tempting not to dwell on the recent death, but you must say something. Most bereaved people are keen to talk about the departed. Nothing is going to make the bereaved feel better but a nice recollection of the deceased is always good. Take a moment to bring one to mind before you speak to them. If you can't think of what to say, 'I'm sorry for your loss' will do just fine. You are unlikely to be able to think of anything to truly comfort but at least try to be thoughtful.

5. Be respectful
It is possible that you had some grievance in the past with the deceased. Now is not the time to mention it. Mentioning money that they owed you is not going to go well either. Instead, consider writing a handwritten letter of happier memories.

6. Let the bereaved speak
They are likely to be awash with emotions and you just need to listen. You can be guided by them as to what they want to talk about.

7. Be practical
Some people like to bring food to the house of a bereaved person who may not be looking after themselves very well. You don't, however, want to overwhelm them or bring something inappropriate. Don't overwhelm a grief-stricken person with elaborate

food that requires intense preparation or flowers which need everyone to hunt around for yet another vase. Easy to eat food and flowers already arranged are best. Check with other members of the family about what would be useful. See if there is anything else you can do to help.

8. Don't stay too long

People in grief need distraction but they also need time to themselves. Make sure you don't overstay your welcome when you visit. This is not a time for them to be thinking about providing you with refreshments.

BURIALS

As soon as death occurs, some one (the trained nurse usually) draws the blinds in the sick-room and tells a servant to draw all the blinds of the house.

Emily Post, *Etiquette*, 1922

(Pause a moment out of respect for Emily)

And on …

People have been burying each other (usually when dead) since before people were actually human. Pop to the Pontnewydd Cave in Denbighshire and, although you can't go in, trust me when I tell you that in 1978 archaeologists discovered dead Neanderthals who had been neatly put away in there about 220,000 years ago.

There are, of course, many ways to say goodbye to someone – in a coffin, urn, embalmed, mummified, frozen, donated body to science, buried at sea, taken to the top of a mountain and fed to vultures, and cannibalism (although that is not a popular option these days). King Tut's elaborate grave is a good example of the trouble people can go to in seeing the dead on their way.

When the philosopher Jeremy Bentham died in 1832 his body, as requested in his will, was dissected as part of a public anatomy lecture. Afterward, the skeleton and head were preserved and stored in a wooden cabinet called the 'Auto-icon', with the skeleton stuffed with hay and dressed in Bentham's clothes. You can see it on public display at the end of the south cloisters in the main building of University College in London. For the 100th and 150th anniversaries of the college, it was brought to the meeting of the College Council, where it was listed as 'present but not voting'.

John Reed, a stagehand who in the first half of the 1800s worked at the Walnut Street Theatre in Philadelphia for more than fifty years, stipulated in his will that he wanted his skull separated from his body, duly prepared, and used to represent the skull of Yorrick in Hamlet. His wish was granted, and the skull is signed by many famous actors of the day who performed in Shakespeare's play.

Sometimes, warriors or servants were buried standing up, eternally ready for action. Mary, I hope you won't need any of this information for many years to come but if you should one day find yourself in charge of seeing that a deceased's departure goes well, then do it with the care you would wish for yourself. Try to fulfil their wishes. It is about showing respect even if they are not around to see it. A date, venue and type of ceremony needs to be organised, and then you need to think about ...

PLANNING THE CEREMONY

1. Check if the deceased had any particular wishes

Some people leave very clear instructions about what they want for their funeral and what they want to happen to their body. Some are more sensible than others. In about 1280 there was a nobleman of the house of Du Chatelet who died leaving instructions that one of the pillars in the church of Neufchateau be hollowed out and his body placed upright in it 'in order that the vulgar may not walk upon me'. Leaving instructions can be helpful to the bereaved although they can't always be pleasant to carry out. When the Marquis of Hastings died in 1826 he left instructions for his right hand to be cut off and buried with his wife so that he might hold hands with her forever. His hand rests in his wife Flora's in the family vault at Loudoun Kirk in Scotland.

2. Try to reflect the deceased's life

This may mean holding a ceremony according to the tenets of a particular religion or having aspects of the event which reflect their profession. In Ghana there are coffin makers who specialise in creating bespoke coffins so that one can be buried in a car, the Statue of Liberty, a lipstick or any other item requested. Arch West was the man who invented the snack, Doritos. When he died his family threw handfuls of them on his coffin.

Notifications

Poor Jud is dead...
The daisies in the dell
Will give out a different smell
Because poor Jud is underneath the ground.

Oscar Hammerstein II (1895–1960), from the musical *Oklahoma!*

Letting people know the details about a funeral is often done by bush telegraph – phoning, texting or email – as there is usually not a great deal of time. It is common to share funerary rites with those who knew the deceased. People want to attend in order to 'pay their respects'. Enlisting friends or family to help spread the word is common. Some faiths, such as Judaism, require burial to be swift after death so notification has to be by word of mouth. All that is needed is the basic information which will enable the recipient to attend. These are functional announcements not obituaries. If you do send out written notification you don't need a photo of the deceased. More elaborate invitations can be written if there is a memorial service later.

Make sure anyone who ought to know has already been informed of the death

You don't want to surprise anyone close to the deceased by sending them a funeral notice before they've even heard of the death. Phone or speak to everyone in person before you send an invitation. Tell them gently and not in the manner of those lyrics from *Oklahoma!*

Flowers

Some people prefer mourners to give a donation to a particular charity instead. Make a clear request so that people find it easy to do what is wanted.

ATTENDING A FUNERAL

1. Turn up

Sounds very basic, doesn't it, but this is not the time to find you have something else to do.

2. Be exactly on time

Don't be early. This is particularly the case if the service is being held at a crematorium. Crematoriums are very busy places and you could find yourself involved in the departure of someone you never met. If you are gathering at the deceased's house first, again, being early is not appropriate. The relatives will need all the time they can have to hold themselves together. Don't be late. Even though the person is dead and not going anywhere, people like these things done promptly. The service will start without you.

If you are late, wait at the back until there is a moment you can slip into a seat near the door.

3. Dress appropriately

Furs are not admissible in widows' first mourning, though very dark sealskin and astrachan can be worn when the dress is changed.

Sylvia's *Home Journal: For Home Reading and Home Use,
of Tales, Stories, Fashion, and Needlework*, 1879

There used to be very strict rules about clothing for mourners but matters are generally more relaxed now. Check whether the bereaved or their family have asked for a specific dress code. They may want you to wear the deceased's favourite colour. Black is not essential but you must dress smartly out of respect. Shorts and sandals, for example, unless specifically requested, would not look great. Ties and clean shoes are a good start for men. Hats are no longer required for women.

4. Try to be no trouble

Sit in the most convenient seat. This is not a time to squeeze in so you can sit with someone you haven't seen for ages.

5. Turn off your phone

That pesky phone has been a lifelong nuisance, hasn't it? Leave it in your car or at home but don't let your Elvis ringtone add further distress to an already tricky day.

6. Do as asked

This is not the time to quibble about anyone's faith. Follow the ritual they feel is appropriate. Perform any favours asked of you, such as a reading, even if you don't have the same beliefs as the bereaved.

7. Check your mirth meter

This may not be the time for lots of jokes and gossip. Check the mood. Humour is not out of place at a funeral but it needs to be appropriate and not everyone is a brilliant judge of that.

When the great writer Thomas Hardy died there was a public demand for him to be buried in Westminster Abbey. His wife, Florence, however, wanted him buried at Stinsford churchyard in Dorset so a compromise was reached. Hardy's heart was removed so that it might go to Dorset and the body to the Abbey. The story goes that the doctor who performed this surgery left the heart in a dish when he had removed it and went to do something else. When he returned he found his cat had eaten part of Hardy's heart. I don't know if it's true, but one popular end to this tale is that the cat was killed, too, and buried alongside the remains of the heart in Stinsford. If the guests at his funeral knew this I can only imagine it was hard to refrain from talking about it.

8. Do be accepting

How the bereaved wish to say goodbye to their loved one is up to them. If they want to sing and wear bright colours or tell jokes it is not for you to disapprove.

9. Don't blame the deceased for their own death

This is not the time to be smug about your gym membership or excellent blood pressure.

10. Do remember all the rules about alcohol

There may well be an open bar but now is not the time.

Private funerals

If people say they are having a 'Private' funeral that means you are not invited, so don't go.

Cremation

Some religions have very strict views on cremation. Hindus believe that cremation is essential as the burning releases the soul from the body, while Roman Catholics frown on cremation out of respect for the body as a symbol of human life. Check you know who believes what. The rules for attending a cremation are the same as for a funeral. Behave yourself. Have respect.

THE WILL

Death is not the end. There remains the litigation over the estate.

Ambrose Bierce (1842–c. 1913), American author

It is part of the human condition that people wish to control matters even after they have died. Wills have been around for a very long time. In Genesis you find Jacob's will, which is one of the earliest mentioned in literature. He died in Egypt aged 147 so he probably had a lot of stuff by then which needed sorting. Noah divided his landed possessions, which was basically the globe, between his three sons. He left out the United States because it hadn't been discovered yet.

You can do what you like in a will. People have left money to goldfish, to carp at Fontainebleau, parrots, many horses, greyhounds, drinking fountains and so on. Jonathan Jackson of Columbus, Ohio, who died in 1880, left money and plans for a cat's home which included dormitories, a canteen, areas for 'conversation' and an auditorium where the cats where to gather for an hour every day to listen to a man play the accordion.

When a Vermont tanner called John Bowman died in 1891 he left a $50,000 trust fund for the maintenance of his twenty-one-room mansion in Cuttingsville and for dinner for four to be prepared every night. His wife and two daughters had prede-ceased him and believed they would all be reincarnated together. The dinner was to welcome them all back, and it is alleged that it was served nightly to an empty room until the money ran out in 1950. If you drive past his old house you can see a life-sized statue of John – carrying a wreath and a key and looking devas-tated – outside the door of the mausoleum where his family were buried.

If someone has left you out of their will

Get over it.

My lovely Mary, I hope that death does not trample through your vineyard too often and that you have the longest and happiest of lives. I don't know where anyone goes after they take their last breath. One rather practical and yet beautiful thought is to consider stardust. The human body is made of water, proteins, fats and mineral nutrients which in turn consist of chemical elements such as hydrogen, oxygen, carbon and nitrogen. These atom types are all created during a supernova explosion. Most of what we are made of was created inside stars and distributed by stellar winds into space as stardust. We came from the stars and now, perhaps, to the stars we return.

Much love

Sandi

EPILOGUE

WHERE GOOD MANNERS ARE BAD

Dear Mary

I have got all the way to the end, you've been terribly patient and now I am going to tell you that sometimes having manners is a really bad idea. Annoying but true. There is a completely bonkers drawing by the French obstetrician, Jacques-Pierre Maygnier, from 1822, which shows a gynaecologist examining a woman. She is not in 'stirrups' or even naked. Rather she is standing wearing a long skirt while the doctor kneels before her putting his hands up her skirt to feel her genitalia but not look at it. This is clearly manners gone mad. Fortunately the medical profession has moved on, but there are still times when being too polite is a bad idea. There are even times for bad behaviour.

The downside to manners

Sadly, etiquette has sometimes been used to keep people in their place. Louis XIV, for example, with his wretched tickets, helped keep his nobles of France in check by making daily adherence to his edicts about how to behave and what to wear very complicated. Everyone spent so long mastering court etiquette that they didn't have time to plot against the king. All the rules revolved around the king's daily routine and some of them were bizarre. For example, no one was allowed to knock on the king's door. They had to scratch very gently with the nail of the little finger of their left hand.

Some people, the crawlers of their day, grew that fingernail especially long to prove quite how devoted they were to his majesty. Louis XIV used etiquette as a social weapon and sometimes a group will adopt some superficial mannerisms for no other reason than snobbery. This is not kind and is actually very bad manners.

When following the rules tips over into bad manners

Some of the greatest rudeness arises when someone insists on sticking to a particular rule even though the circumstances call for some flexibility. I was once the 'celebrity guest' at a charity match at a golf club in Richmond in Surrey. It was not a good day for golf as it poured with rain throughout. Nevertheless, I threw myself into the event with gusto. I blew up balloons before we started, I did several interviews with the press throughout the day lauding both the club and the charity, and I played stolidly through the downpour. On returning to the clubhouse I was hungry and wet but I realised that I had only brought trainers to change into. The club did not allow trainers in the dining room and I had to go home without being either fed or offered a hot drink. It was astonishing. No one seemed aware that this might have been a good day for the club to overlook my shoes.

So remember your Top Cs of manners and keep in the back of your mind that

Rigidity to Rules can lead to Rudeness

It's also worth bearing in mind . . .

1. Not to keep saying sorry

There is a difference between being appropriately apologetic and turning into a doormat. If you make a mistake, say you are sorry and then move on. Being too sorry can be annoying.

2. Don't stay quiet if something needs saying

Complaining about bad service, food, treatment is not bad manners. It's the way in which you do it that matters. It is far worse to say nothing and not give the person providing the service, food, etc., a chance to put something right.

3. Don't be too stoic

The British have a wonderful reputation for stoicism, and not being a whinger is a good thing. Don't, however, take this to extremes. Don't be the person who, failing to get medical attention because they don't want to 'bother the doctor', dies; or the person who doesn't respond when someone is rude to them; or the person who puts their own life in danger because they don't like to say 'no'. Look after yourself.

So although occasionally sticking to the rules can have a downside, mostly manners are marvellous. I began the book with a story from the photographer, Patrick Lichfield, so it seems neat to finish with one. Patrick was born in 1939 and was a very small boy during the Second World War. He lived in London, which was heavily bombed. He explained the notion of the 'stiff upper lip' to me by relating an occasion when he had been taken out to tea by his nanny. They were in a very smart restaurant when a bomb exploded nearby and part of the ceiling fell in. All the customers, including Patrick, dived under their tables. When the dust settled Patrick slowly reappeared from beneath the table to find Nanny still sitting drinking her tea. 'Nanny, was that a bomb?' he enquired, wide-eyed. 'Yes dear,' replied Nanny. 'Elbows off the table.'

Well, that's it, I think. I mean there are lots of events which I haven't thought of which will arise, but I hope I have covered the basics. Having said that manners are occasionally not a good idea, those occasions are rare. I think of the words of the great silent film star Lillian Gish who said 'You can get through life with bad manners, but it's easier with good manners.' I like you so very much and I want everyone else to feel the same. Having good manners will help.

Much love

Sandi